James Anthony Froude, Thomas Carlyle

Reminiscences of my Irish Journey in 1849

James Anthony Froude, Thomas Carlyle
Reminiscences of my Irish Journey in 1849
ISBN/EAN: 9783744761048
Printed in Europe, USA, Canada, Australia, Japan
Cover: Foto ©Andreas Hilbeck / pixelio.de

More available books at **www.hansebooks.com**

REMINISCENCES

OF

MY IRISH JOURNEY

IN 1849.

BY

THOMAS CARLYLE.

London:
SAMPSON LOW, MARSTON, SEARLE, & RIVINGTON,
CROWN BUILDINGS, 188, FLEET STREET.
1882.

[All rights reserved.]

PREFACE.

In Mr. Carlyle's journal for 1849 are the two following entries:—

"*May*, 17, 1849.—Am thinking of a tour in Ireland: unhappily have no call of *desire* that way, or any way, but am driven out somewhither (just now) as by the point of bayonets at my back. Ireland really *is* my problem; the breaking point of the huge suppuration which all British and all European society now is. Set down in Ireland, one might at least feel, '*Here* is thy problem: In God's name what wilt thou do with it?'"

"*November* 11, 1849.—Went to Ireland as

foreshadowed in the last entry; wandered about there all through July: have half forcibly recalled all my remembrances, and thrown them down on paper since my return. Ugly spectacle: sad health: sad humour: a thing unjoyful to look back upon. The whole country figures in my mind like a ragged coat; one huge beggar's gaberdine, not patched or patchable any longer: far from a joyful or beautiful spectacle."

The remembrances thus set down are here printed. The MS. is not one of those which were entrusted by Mr. Carlyle to myself. It consists merely of fragmentary notes, to which he attributed no importance. He gave it to Mr. Neuberg, who was then acting as his secretary; Mr. Neuberg gave it to the late Mr. Thomas Ballantyne; by Mr. Ballantyne it was sold to a Mr. Anderson, from whom it came into the hands of the present publishers. They being in possession of the property, were free to do with it as they pleased; but they were good enough to ask my opinion as to the propriety of giving it to the world, and I saw no objection to their doing so. The Irish problem has not been solved since Mr. Carlyle's visit, nor has it been made more easy of solution by the policy of successive ministries, which has been precisely opposite to what Mr. Carlyle would have himself recommended. His remarks, rough and hasty as they are, cannot be injurious, and may possibly be useful. Nothing which he wrote has been altered, and nothing has been suppressed. I have corrected the Press as far as I have been able, but the handwriting is more than usually intricate. A few words are almost illegible, and I have not ventured on conjectural emendations.

J. A. FROUDE.

ONSLOW GARDENS,
April 22, 1882.

REMINISCENCES OF MY IRISH JOURNEY IN 1849.

CHELSEA, 4th Oct., 1849.—I will now, my long confused wayfarings of the Summer being ended, endeavour to write down with all despatch what I can remember of them. After much sorting of paper-rubbish, reading over of all the Irish letters to my wife and kindred, and in some measure clearing the decks (not for "action" yet, alas, no, no!) set about this, which I partly consider a clearing of my own mind, as some kind of "preparation for action." *Faxit.*

Reminiscences of my Irish Journey.

Saturday, 30th June, 1849.—After endless "agonies of preparation," natural to a poor stationary sedentary, biliary, and otherwise much bewildered mortal, about 8 in the morning I got on board the Chelsea steamer here, at the Cadogan Pier; left my poor Wife gazing sorrowfully after me, and, in a close, damp-sunny morning, was wafted swiftly down the river. Memory now is a blank nightmare till I reach the wooden platform swinging on the river just above London Bridge, north side, and call earnestly for some boatman to take my luggage and me "to the Athlone, at Alderman Stairs." Boatman comes, a ragged, lean greasy and sooty creature, with hurried toilsome eyes and shallow *shelf* chin—" a wholesome small nature, terribly beaten upon and stunted"— who cheerfully takes me in; zealously descends the river with me, tide against him; whisks his way like a needle thro' innumerable impediments of ships, rafts, barges; sweating, panting, eyes looking still more toilsome, jacket doffed, shelf-chin still more protruded;

and at half-past nine, reaches the Athlone, a dingy dirty-looking Dublin steamer (but a steamer and mode of travel I had chosen *against* my lazy *wishes*, and in obedience to my insights and determinations); and, after rowing round (steward or third mate at first refusing to let down the steps) puts me on board—takes 1*s.* 6*d.* with protest, the double his fare, and splashes away again about his business. There am I on board.

Steamer lying all, to an unexpected degree, as if in a kind of greasy sleep. £2 fare demanded by some landsman interested, seems the liveliest fact. Canaille of various kinds, Irish by look, getting itself located in the fore-deck; one yellow-faced, roughish, very slight-made Irish figure in cab half-drunk fixes my attention, by his endless talk to Stewards &c. seemingly about nothing at all or next to nothing: a sorrowful phenomenon often confirmed afterwards. Half-pay Serjeant looking figure,—clean old Lancashire physiognomy of fifty (old Indian soldier, now at Falmouth, as I learned afterwards) is talking insipidities about the news from the papers, I forget what. Other figures—the more spectral in my memory, somewhat like spectral flies in a spectral gluepot! I was very sick in body, perhaps still more so in soul; and had, by no means, a lively mirror of attention to hold up to them. At 10 o'clock, nevertheless, with unexpected precision, a bell rang, the steam mechanism began growling, and we jumbled forth on our way.

To the river-mouth I remember little with distinctness; the day had settled into grey; with more than enough of east-wind now that our own velocity was added to it. The brick-chaos and ship-and-boat-chaos of big London till after Greenwich lies across my remembrance like an ugly indistinct *smear*, full of noise and confusion, no figure distinct in it. Passengers, one after one, came on board; at Greenwich a great many Soldiers "recruits and invalids" Irish both, the latter from India, and " bad subjects" mostly, as I learned afterwards,—these came on board at Gravesend in great number, drunk many of them, with or without officers (*without* it afterwards turned out); a nasty sight rather. Pilot-boats hooked themselves astern of us, and went shoving thro' the foam; sometimes as many as 4 boats at once: " pilots looking out for a job,"—favoured by the Steamers. A tall antelope or panther figure in red coat (about Gravesend, I think) misses the proper boarding-place from his boat; steps into one of these pilot-boats, cool he amid the tumult of noises and splashing of spray; and twists gallantly aloft over the stern; dashes the spray from self and papers, and with a brisk calmness which I could not but admire, stept smiling forwards to his place, the fore-deck: a corporal of foot; commander he, as I found, of the broken military there. An exceedingly tall lank simple-looking Irish gentleman came on board thereabouts too, whom I afterwards named to myself the "Irish Toots" (see Dickens). A very short wellconditioned cockney-looking gentleman had likewise come. I took him for the Captain of these Majesty's forces of ours; but found afterwards he was a tourist, "looking at all the capital Cities," Paris last year, Dublin this; he had a small sea-store (from which I guessed a wife too); his big blue eyes, silly as he was, had at times a beautiful sorrow in them while he sat silent in the evening on deck for a while; a rough pugface—tamed into perfect peaceable politeness, had in it an air of limited rationality, veracity and English wholesomeness, which pleased me. But I must get on! Somewhere on the river a big fat Englishman of 50 stept on board, burly, black, pock-marked, one eye shut (seemingly out, but it proved to be *in* too, on occasion): some trader (one would have hoped, in *bacon* and *edibles*) to the Plymouth region,

I afterwards found. One other cabin passenger, *where* entering I noticed not, was an elderly Lancashire or Cumberland man, you could not say of what quality below a gentn.; feeble-minded, good-humoured, his old wrinkly face grew quite blown-out at last, the eyes almost shut up, by inflammatory regimen of whiskey &c. and want of sleep, before the voyage ended. I did not in the least hate, yet how little either, did I pity this poor old man. Alas, wrapt up in our own black cares (which we ought to conquer, and keep moderately conquered, if we stood to our post), shut up the soul of man from feeling for his brother,—surely an ignoble state! Let this suffice for our ship's loading. I remember very vaguely Erith, much more so Southend or rather the *name* of "Southend and its long Pier," (a cockney bathing-place). I have a dim *tint* of grey-green country and spectral objects enough there rushing past me all that day and afternoon. Our Captain, an excellent, civil, able, old Welshman, kept aloft on the platform; very obliging when you spoke to him. I went twice there with a cigar, looked down into the sea of Irish rabble, and began to decipher type-faces of the Irish. The "light boats," we passed near to two or three of them; the dreariest objects I ever in this world saw; the "Girder" "Tongue" &c. on their several shoals of those names; must keep a light burning at night; the two men have no function else whatever; I suppose they can *eat* terribly, and sleep nearly the whole day. Their boats were bobbing and capering in the wild surf; narrow was the share otherwise these poor fellows had of this Universe. It is a wild expanse of shoals and channels, this Thames mouth. I had never been on that side of it, at least never in daylight, having usually in former voyages passed by the Nore. Of Broadstairs and Ramsgate, nothing but a tremulous cloudy shadow remains. Ditto of Deal. I saw Walmer Castle, Duke of Wellington's, looking down on us with wings of planted wood; less memorably some big Hotel, perhaps more than one, its windows glittering in the bleared windy sunset,—not beautiful to me they, or anything, in that sad mood. Dover (lived at, 24 years before, one autumn) looked grim enough in the twilight; I could recognise almost nothing of my old localities, the new " entrance of the tunnel" was not recogniseable except as a small blotch. How I took tea &c. and went to bed is quite *abolished* from recollection; too well can I recollect the *snoring* of my one-eyed provision friend,— whose *eating* at tea, whole chickens and plates of ham vanishing before him, I do now recollect! Also that I got up, probably about midnight; was *told* we were opposite Brighton, but could see no token of that or of anything but a dim flat coast with some kind of luminous gleam all along where sea met land; whereupon I had to smoke a pipe, and descend to my lair again. Cyclops snoring still more effectively now—seldom or never heard such snoring, which was not a *stream*, diastole and systole, but a *whirlpool* rather, or system of whirlpools, bottomless maelstroms and sandy syrtis conjoined (ah me!) for the man was nearly suffocated by closed curtains and by vanished plates of ham. I have a dim but certain recollection of jumping out of my bed or drawer at last, indignantly dashing his curtains open, with some passionate demand to "*cease* that beastly gurgling and gluddering, in the name of all the devils!" Whereby at least my heavy Provisional friend did awake; and I fell asleep and heard no more of him for that night. Poor fellow; not a bad creature, after all; there seemed a kind of healthy banter in him, a merry vivid eye; probably an *excellent* dealer in bacon, praiseworthy as a British citizen of 1849; but he did eat excessively, and his snoring was to me at once hateful and terrible,—poor fellow after all!

Sunday morning (1 July) at 7 came on deck: beautifully sunny morning, Isle of Wight, Ventnor region lying close at hand, and the ship motionless waiting for the turn of the tide—wind had gone round from east to west in the night: we hung for about an hour with little, at first with next to no motion, opposite that southwest region of the little Island. The special localities, none of which were known to me beforehand, I did not get committed to memory. A straggling hamlet (perhaps about Dunnose, I can't now find on the map any name that fixes itself as the name then given me) with a kind of bay and clayey unbeautiful coasts, this stood distinct; less so other straggling human objects; and now only Ventnor itself figures as absorbing the whole vivid past of the scene. A steepish slope, very green but rather treeless; houses and little gardens sprinkled over a good part of it, connected by oblique paths; grass-surface very beautiful everywhere, shrubberies apparently flourishing; a pleasant group of dwellings hung out there against the morning sun,—and one of them, I knew not which, had been John Sterling's last dwelling! I looked intently, with many thoughts. Bonchurch not visible now—had it been? I knew also (what was curious to think of) that John Forster, little dreaming of my whereabout, was in one White's at Bonchurch, down from London that very morning. Far elsewhither was I bound. With eye or with glass, looking never so intently I could discover no human or even living figure; which proves perhaps that our distance was greater than the short distance it appeared to be. "Toots" very loquacious when he could get a chance, came talking about Dr. McHale of Tuam ("Chuam" he called it) and Nangle of Achil Island;

and how John had " cursed them all with bell, book, and candle " &c. which I shook off, not believing it at all literally in spite of Toots's evident *bona fides*, and wishing indeed to see Ventnor rather than *it*. After Ventnor, talk with the Half-pay Serjt. Major; Wight now flitting faster by us, the ship being under full movement again; of Indian soldiering; mainly about the economics, difficulties &c. of locomotion for armies; but above all things the *prices* of articles in the various markets, allowances of grog—what you could *get*, and pocket or swallow, by your soldiering in India—this was the theme of my half-pay Serjt. A most healthy practical man; simplicity itself, and yet *savoir-faire* enough, tough as leather, and a *stroke* in him (I could see) like that of a quarter staff of *oak*. Man worth remembering, told me of his pensions, promotions, appointment now (to some military charge of a district, I think) at Falmouth: " as good as £100 in all, sir, which is very well, *you* see"; more total absence of *bragging*, nay of self consciousness or of any unwholesome element it was impossible to see or figure. Soldiering like working, in such men; *strong* both ways, as native oak: the strongest kind of men. After Wight, Needles &c. (terribly worn, almost dilapidated and ruinous-ugly looking) had rapidly flowed past,—perhaps before 10 o'clock, the coast left us; Southampton &c. far in the distance, passed unnoticed, and I think I must have taken to read Quaker Pim's book on Ireland which also passed unnoticed. Or perhaps I went to sleep? Probably that *was* it? Yes, in my notebook (pencil) it is marked so "fell asleep on deck a little in the sun towards noon."

N.B.—After 3 days more there is not even a pencil scrap, nothing but the letters to help me to decipher what was the exact day of this or that occurrence still remembered by me.

It turned out now there had a man been *lost* last night. The good old Captain so reported it. On Saturday evening, most of the poor Irish wretches of " invalids " got more or less completely drunk ; some of them even on entering, had needed no completing. One of them a lean, angry, misguided, entirely worthless looking creature, age perhaps 40, came staggering upon the quarter-deck, and made a turn there : turn nearly completed, he came right upon the captain who of course ordered him off,—which order, tho' given mildly enough the poor drunk wretch felt to be insulting to his honour, and swore fiercely not to comply with. A scuffle had ensued (Captain's hand got " twisted ") : all of us started up to conjure the poor wretch &c.; he did then turn off, abashed, perhaps repentant, had taken more drink for consolation ; was " last seen about midnight " : it was now he that was never to be seen more ! The Irish physiognomies I

studied often from the upper platform:
besides my yellow friend with the cap, I
had made out some five or six type-physiog-
nomies, which I could recognize as specimens
of Irish *classes* of faces: there was the
angry-bewildered, for instance the poor
wretch that went overboard, or a still better
yet left on board, a lean withered show of a
creature with hanging brows, droop nose,
mouth corners drooping, chin narrow, narrow,
eyes full of sorrow and rage; " I have a right
to be here, sir, I want my ration!" said he
once. There was there a blonde big tiger-face
(to whom I lent a light for his pipe); this is
of mixed breed, I think a north country face:
noble possibility quite marred. Irish sailor
at the helm in wig and storm hat; bulky,
with aquiline face and closed mouth, wild
cunning little eye: like Jock McDonald of my
early years. Ah me! These faces are still
very clear to me; and were I a painter, I
could draw them; others, one or two, not

thought of again till now, have got erased; I was struck in general with the air of faculty *misbred*, and gone to waste, or more or less " excellent possibility much marred," in almost all these faces. The man had found himself so enveloped in conditions which he deemed unfair, which he had revolted against, but had not been able to conquer, that he had so to speak, *lost his way;* a sorry sight, the *tragedy* of each of these poor men; but here too surely is a " possibility"; if the Irish faculty be good, you *can* breed it, put it among conditions which *are* fair or at least fairer.

" Portland Bill ": it was on awakening from one of my deck sleeps, well on in the afternoon that this object, a muddy-beached little Island, I found,—perhaps an Island only at high tide :—shaped rather like a battle *bill* —was that the origin of the name? From this point the Coast continued our neighbour again; by degrees Dorsetshire passed, and then Devonshire with its gnarled rocks (as if they were whinstone or limestone, and scotch rocks) winded rapidly off, as the evening sank—viewless now, damp, and rather windy, as we were running into the teeth of the breeze. Many caves, gnarled promontories, rock islets; trim houses and fields, no human creature visible: a silent English sabbath country,—like the dream of a sabbath. Mate, of whom anon, points out Plymouth light in the thickening dusk; past 10 we make the light: Breakwater with its *red* lamp, with its sudden calm of sea, and tumult of boats;— we were in some most dark, strait place, with rain beginning, and they called it Plymouth Harbour. Toots's talk to me, while the bustle went on, about an Irish lord (just dead?) and his brother, transcendent blackguards, beautiful man, dance or dinner of innumerable improper-females in London once—pity rather that I have forgotten that: but of

Toots who could do anything but forget? Smooth-flowing shallow shameless river of talk; always in one or two minutes, when I could not bodily get away from him, my thoughts slid far away. These transcendent Irish lords were connected, somehow by marriage, with the late Duke of Gordon. Of my night in this harbour there remains yet sad memorial; in a scrawl of a letter begun about midnight to my wife! Enough here to record the stages or chief epochs: 1. To bed very sleepy. Toots and the Lancashire Non-significant, talking serious jargon for about an hour in the cabin, wouldn't let me; I remember, the poor cockney tourist had been asking " for a pen," remembered Post Office *here*, and started up to *write*, by way of deliverance from that car-torment:—2. Writing with ear-torment still *worse* near at hand, my Provisional friend (O Heaven I thought *he* had been gone, never to snore more) stept in, evidently full of food and porter; at sight of him I start, can write no farther; lock up my writing case, wait impatiently that Toots and Non-significant would end. 3. Try bed again; can't at all. Toots and Non-significant stumble in, rain patters on the deck, Provisional friend takes to *snoring*—" blubber—gurgle—gludder!" I start up and don my clothes; find in the cabin too a poor under-steward snoring, loudly but humanly, and have not the heart to awaken him. Uncertain what to do, fly on deck, smoke (under my umbrella), try *not* to despair; find at last a side cabin with nothing in it but rubbish of clothes, a sofa and an open window; fling myself down there, thanking Heaven, and fall sound asleep—till 8 next morning.

Monday 2nd July.

All busy when I came on deck; sunny morning, boxes, bales, persons getting or got on board; soon sail; have seen nothing of Plymouth, see little even of the harbour except confusion of ropes and ships;—size of it guessable at less than I expected. Tract of town (Catwater they called it?) stretching back on the right as we sailed *out;* buildings like public storehouses, or official houses, farther down; two neat women step hurriedly on board there; *mis*venturous Irish-women, giving up their plan of emigration to Australia, and cowering back to Ennis in Clare, as I afterwards learned; sisters, Misses Hewit by name. Breakwater a stone glacis, with light-tower (perhaps cannon-tower too) and small esplanade at the end, some frigates scattered about; it was Plymouth sound; pretty enough in the summer morning after such a night. Various new figures now on board; new prey to Toots. I spoke to none; hoped they would leave at Falmouth where we were to call. Sick gentleman in big wicker cradle lay on the deck; poor fellow!

"paralytic in the lower extremities," going to Dublin for surgery, attended only by a rough clown of a servant; his eyes looked mild and patient, tho' sad; intelligent white face; age probably about 35; they shifted him round out of the sun; not to embarrass him, we had to forbear looking at his cradle or him.

Cornish coast, as that of Devonshire had been, gnarled rocky; indented all along, harbour and sound (when once you had "opened" it) at the bottom of each little bay " Pol "— something or other, when you asked the name. An interesting event to me. Looe: "that is Looe," that strait hardly perceptible crack or notch in the rocks there.—Poor C. Buller, poor old years of his and mine! Fowey-Harbour entrance was marked by white spots, a couple, *painted* on the rocks; not find it otherwise. Toots *preying* on the new comers. "Hum-m-m. Drum-m-m!" with a strong Irish intonation in it. Many trim sloops of one pattern, with red sails and conspicuous label ("P. H. No. 1" &c.? something like that) were nimbly cutting about: "Pilchard-boats, sir!" All busy here, crowded steamer crossed us on the left: pleasure-trip, Falmouth—to the Eddystone probably. Half-pay serjeant did the honours of the coast as we approached his new home; has liberty seemingly of the quarter-deck, but feeds and sleeps in some region of his own. About noon or after, past St. Mawes and on the left past Pendennis,—Falmouth; and moor there "for about an hour"—which proved two hours and more.

I might, had I foreseen that latter fact, have gone ashore to see "Barclay Fox" and Co., if nothing better; nay, I was near going, had my foot on the ladder towards a boat, but in the scrambling tumult gave it up again, and decided to stay and look about me and pensively smoke and consider. John Sterling's house was there too; but nobody could tell me which; tho' one, a brisk young damsel, did point out the warehouse of the Foxes, a big house near the sea. Falmouth might contain 3 or 4 thousand souls (as the look suggested to guess); it hung, pleasantly enough, tho' much too bare-looking, on the slope of the acclivity and down close to the sea; reminded me a little of Kirkcaldy, except that this was squarish in shape, not "a long town" rather a "loose town," as I judged; one street near the sea, main street I suppose, on the *level;* the sloping thoroughfares I judged to be mostly lanes. The country looked bare; the harbour land-locked is beautiful, and if deep must be excellent. Assisted clown to screen the poor invalid gentleman in his cradle from the hot windless sun; fixed up my own umbrella over him, which the clown afterwards told me, in confidential gratitude, was "a graat suppoart"—Sent a card ashore to Fox; admired the clean, sturdy, clear-looking boatmen;

watched their long dangerous loading and disloading. Toots had gone, Provisional friend (O joy !) had gone ; hoped we should now have a stiller time. About two the steam growled again, and we got under way, close to the little pleasant Castle of Pendennis this time, a trim castellated height with trim paths &c. (one company in it, Serjt. half-Pay had said) ; and so again out to the open deep.

Our 2 Irishwomen " from Ennis in Clare" with their clean summer-bonnets (mere clean calico, folded full over paste board, with a tack or two; much admired by me) had come to the quarter-deck ; wished evidently to be spoken to ; were by me, after others of us. Father had been a Lieutenant of foot with pension, mother too with pension; both being dead, resources were all out : parson had advised emigration, "free passage to Australia" was certain if we would deposit £12 in advance ; deposited, sold off, came to Plymouth, found the "free passage" a passage among parish paupers, and shrieked (of course) at the notion of it! Officers had been extremely helpful and polite; got us back, with difficulty, our £12; and here we are, wending our sad way home again! A more distressing story I had not lately heard. For both the women, "ladies" you could not have hesitated even in the poor-house to call them, were clearly of superior faculty and quality: the elder some 45 perhaps, a rugged brave-looking woman; the younger delicate, graceful, and even still beautiful, tho' verging towards middle-age also. The two unfortunates, was there nothing other for them by way of career in the world but this! The younger was quite pleasant company; but at "the Lizard" or earlier began to grow sick, grew ever sicker, and I had to lead her to her place, a horrible den called "Second Cabin," and there leave her sister and her. Ill-nature of the stewardess, tiff between the good old captain and her because of these poor Miss Hewits. "Bring me our basket, pray sir! Stewardess will give it you!" were the last words of the elder from her dark den. Stewardess knew nothing of their basket, not she; old captain awoke from his after-dinner nap, reproached the woman for her greedy hard character, *ordered* her to "know" the basket, which, with very angry tears, assisted by me and my soothing eloquence, the creature at last did. Base, in many cases, under certain aspects, is the mind of man!

The "Lizard point" we would pass before dinner; stormy place of cliffs, high cliffs rough water; I found that in shape it did resemble somewhat the head of a Lizard,— at least on the western sides it does. We were past the "souther"most land of Britain then; but the tossing of the water did *not* abate as promised; the evening light glared wild and sad upon the solitary sea, to the Land's-end, that was the word now. Coast still high and all rock; Land's-end stretching out black ahead; it was towards sunset when we actually reached it; passed it round the lighthouse at the distance perhaps of a mile. The wildest most impressive place I ever saw on the coasts of Britain. A lighthouse rises on a detached rock some considerable space ahead; many detached rocks, of a haggard skeleton character, worn haggard by the wild sea, are scattered about between the lighthouse and end of the firm cliff; that cluster, where the lighthouse is, had seemed to me like the ruins of a Cathedral for some time. Very wild and grim, impressive in itself and as the notablest of British capes. A farmhouse called by sailors "First and last" stands very near to the extremity; farther round to the west are villages and many houses visible "mining village" you are told; the promontory itself is among the highest I have seen (much higher than St. Bees I thought); sheer and black. A boat or two, poor specks of piscatory human art, were seen rocking and paddling among the angry skeleton rocks in these ever-vexed waters; where they were to land, or how get up to "First and last" one didn't well see. But here at last is the spectre of the mixed Cathedral,—a lighthouse among haggard sea-beat rocks, namely; and we are *round* the Land's-end, getting round towards the western side of it, and had better look well our *last*. The sunshine now went *out*, angry breeze blew colder from dark cloudy skies,—baddish night, probably? Some poor laboring ship, with patched sails and not otherwise of prosperous aspect met us just past the lighthouse, borne into the grim evening, it on its way, we on ours; and the Land's-end was among the things that had been; "standing for the Tuscar, sir!"—Tuscar Light on the coast of Wexford, 130 miles off. And so the evening and the morning had been a new day.

As there was nothing to be seen on deck but the dim tumult of sea and sky, I suppose I must have gone early to bed: I can remember shutting my little cabin door, (for the harsh stewardess, in hope probably of a shilling, had volunteered to make a bed for me in the place where I had found refuge the night before) with a satisfied feeling, and turning in with great hope: but, alas, it proved far otherwise. My first experience in the new bed was a jolt that nearly threw me out: the wind had risen, was still rising; the steamer pitched, rolled, tumbled, creaked and growled: doors banging, men's feet and voices sounding, and the big sea booming and roaring: not a wink of sleep could be had all night, hardly could one's place in bed be maintained. Some time, perhaps between 3 and 4 I went on deck to smoke; a wild wet stormy dimness everywhere;

the mate dripping from every angle of his face and person—with thin wet shoes on, I remember—approached my shelter, talking sea stoicisms to me, admitting that it was a roughish night: noticeable fellow this; very civil, very good-humoured, sliding about (for he *trailed* his limbs and feet with thin shoes) to put this and that detail in order always; voice thin, creaky, querulous—hesitatory, and as if it couldn't be troubled to speak; a rocking, sliding, innocent-hearted " sea-pedant " (as such I had classed him); with lips drawn in, puckered brow, and good humoured eyes *pretending* to be wearier than they were; came from the Medway, had been wrecked, traded to Aberdeen, was now puddling about in these seas;—may he prosper, poor fellow! I flung myself next on the sofa, under miscellaneous wrappage, and did then get some stony sleep till the morning fairly broke.

Tuesday 3rd July.

On deck between 8 and 9, all hands looking out for "the Tuskar" when doing nothing else; old captain and a wretched passenger or two trying to *walk* the quarter-deck (impossible for any *two*-footed land animal); big sheets of spray dashing over them from time to time A wild grey tumult; sight and sound everywhere of the rather dismal sort in sea and in sky. One ship or perhaps two at various times visible; elsewhere no Tuskar, no motion that was not of the *chaotic* powers. Sailors made a wave or motion or sound of some sort from the platform, Captain too looked; Tuskar at last! In a few instants more I also could see it; white pillar or tower rising steady amid the tumult of the waters, strange and welcome; some 12 miles off, they said. We turned now gradually to the right: for Arklow head, for

Wicklow do., then was Dublin itself to come. Wind, as we turned *from* it on our new course, grew softer somewhat and water smoother, but all day it was gusty, very uncomfortable and too cold. The poor sick gentleman had passed the night on deck, his cradle well screened under tarpaulins; and didn't seem much hurt by the rough weather. Lancashire Non-significant, who took a little punch perhaps too often, seemed greatly out of sorts; his poor face red as vermilion in parts, and swollen as if you had blown up all its old wrinkles with wind;—poor devil; yet he ate again at breakfast, and made no complaint, took nothing amiss.

"Wexford Harbour," visible only as a blank on the line of coast, was a mere tradition to us. Wexford and Wicklow hills (I supposed about Eniscorthy and Ferns) many common-place-looking hills of moderate height and complex arrangement now visible. Vinegar Hill, a peaked flat cone, conspicuous enough among the others. Thought of the "Battle of Vinegar Hill," but not with interest, with sorrow rather and contempt; one of the ten times ten thousand futile fruitless "battles" this brawling unreasonable people has fought,—the saddest of distinctions to them among peoples! In Heaven's name learn that "revolting" is not the trade which will profit you. The unprofitablest of all trades, if you *exceed* in it; In Heaven's name either be at peace, or else try to fight with some chance of success! "Hill of Tarah" visible too, of conical shape; but not the historical illustrious Tara,—that is in Meath, I think; tho' that too is but moderately "illustrious" to me.

Arklow Town I didn't see at all; understood there was next to no town, but remembered "Wooden Ludlow's" adventure there, and could have liked to take some picture of the ground with me. Wicklow head, beautiful trim establishment of a light-house there, properly *three* towers (one or else two of them having proved wrong built), accurately whitewashed, walled in, with paths &c., a pleasure to look at upon the brown crag. These generally like that of Devonshire or the *lower* forms of Scotch coast; interior not ill-cultivated; houses trim enough from the distance, fields fenced and some small stragglings of plantation even. Behind Wicklow Head, in a broad shallow bay looking rather *bleared*, found Wicklow Town, kept looking at it as we sailed northward right away from it; lies in a hollow on the *southern* side of the Bay screened by Wicklow head from the east winds—rather a feeblish kind of County Town; chapels, a steeple, slate roofs, thin cloud of smoke; perhaps 2 or towards 3 thousand inhabitants, as I judged. In all these seas we saw no ship, absolutely none at all but one Wicklow Fishing sloop, of the same form but quite rusty and out of repair, as the Cornish Pilchard-sloops of yesterday ;—alas one, & in this state of ineffectuality. A big steamer farther on, making from Dublin towards "Bristol" (I think our captain said); this and a pilot boat *not* employed by us; except these three we saw no other ships at all in those Irish seas that day. Wonderful & lamentable! chorus all my Irish friends; and grope for their pikes to try and mend it! Bray Head I had seen before; and Bray, but couldn't make my recollections correspond. Beautiful suburban country by the shores there, on the Dublin side. Works of Wicklow Railway, hanging over the sea, I remember, probably about Bray Head. Afternoon sinking lower, wind cold, bleary, loud; no dinner till one got to Dublin: wish we were there. Dublin Bay at last; Kingstown with its small *exotic* rows of villas hanging over the saltwater; Dalkey Islet, with ruined church, close on the other side of us. Kingstown Harbour; huge square basin within granite moles, few ships, small business in it; wild wind was tossing some filament of steam about (mail steamer, getting ready I suppose for Holyhead), and the rest was idle vacancy. Long lines of granite embankment, a noble channel with docks, *miles* of it (there seemed to me), and no ship in it, no human figure on it, the genius of vacancy alone possessing it! Will "be useful some day" I suppose? The look of it, in one's own cold wretched humour, was rather sad.—Dublin Harbour at last; a few ships actually moored here, along the quays nearest to the city. Tumult, as usual; our key was on the north bank. Miss Hewits came up, specially begged me not to leave *their* luggage once on shore till they themselves came with the remainder of it: did so, tho' little able to wait; was hardly ever in a more *deplorable* state of body than even now. Despatched the Miss Hewits; got into a cab myself escaping from the unutterable hurlyburly. "Imperial Hôtel, Sackville Street!"—and was safely set down there, in wind and dust, myself a mass of dust and inflammatory ruin, about 6 or 7 in this evening of Tuesday July 3.—What a pleasure to get fairly washed, and into clean linen and clothes, once more! small wholesome dinner in the ground storey; fine roomy well-ordered place: but, alas, at the Post Office there was no admittance, "all shut at 7." I had to take that disappointment, and instead of receiving letters write letters.

Imperial-Hotel people, warned I suppose by Fitzgerald (Miss Purcell the proprietress's nephew) had brightened up into enthusiastic smiles of welcome at sound of my name: all was done for me then that human waiterage in the circumstances could do; I had a brisk-eyed deft Irish youth by way of special attendant, really a clever, active, punctual youth, who seemed as if he would have run to the world's end for me at lifting of my finger: he got me cloakpins (my little bedroom the "quietest" they had, wanted such); bath tubs, attended to my letters, clothes, messages, waited on me like a familiar fairy. Could they have got me into a room really "quiet," where I might have really slept, *all* had been well there. But that was not possible; not there, nor anywhere else in inns. One's "powers of observation" act under sad conditions, if the nerves are to be continually in a shatter with want of sleep and what it brings! Under that sad condition, as of a gloomy pressure of waking nightmare, were all my Irish operations, of observation or other, transacted; no escape from it; take it silently therefore, *say* nothing more of it, but do the best you may under it as under a law of fate.

About 10 at night, still writing letters, I received "John O'Hagan's" visit; a note from Duffy,[1] who was dining there, had lain waiting for me before—brisk innocent

[1] Duffy, the present Sir Charles Gavan Duffy.

modest young barrister, this John O'Hagan;[2] Duffy's sister-in-law did by no manner of means *let* rooms; so her offer of one, indicated in Duffy's note, had to be at once declined: Duffy himself "would be here in half an hour". Wrote on to my mother or to Jane: Duffy came soon after the time set; drank a "glass of lemonade" from me, I a glass of punch; took my letters of introduction home with him to scheme out a route, gave me a road *series* "drive here first, then there, then &c." for Dublin introductions on the morrow; and after a silent pipe I tumbled into bed.

Wednesday 4th July.

Breakfast in the Public room: considerable company; polite all, and less of noise

[2] John O'Hagan is the present Judge O'Hagan, chief of the Irish Land Commission

among them than when I was formerly there: arrangem^(ts.) all perfect; "toasted bacon", coffee, toast, all right and well served—No letters for me at the Post-Office! strange, but no help. Car ("a shilling an hour") about noon (I think) to go and deliver my introductions; *got* a body of letters just as I was stepping out on this errand: all right, I hope, Post master mistaken before![3] M'Donnel of the national schools, "engaged"; very well; to Board of Works, Poor-law Power not come; Larcom just coming, read my *letters* in his room, go *away* then as he has not yet got his business done.[4] In Merrion Square D^(r.) Stokes *in:* clever, energetic, but squinting, rather fierce, sinister-looking man, —at least some dash of that suspectible in him: to dine there, nevertheless, to-morrow evening—D^(r.) Kennedy not at home, Sir R. Kane d^(o.) (out of town); Sir Duncan Mac-

[3] See Alex. MacDonnel, the Chief Commissioner of Education.

[4] Colonel Larcom, head of the Ordnance Survey.

gregor, found him, an excellent old Scotchman, soldierly, open, genial, sagacious: Friday night to dine with him;[5] left my other military letters there, and drove to M*rs.* Callan's; (Duffy's sister-in-law);—had missed Pim the Quaker before, "in London;" left Forster's letter, declining to see the other members of the firm just now. Long talk with Mrs. Callan, D*r.* C., and M*rs.* Duffy; Duffy in his room ill of slight cold. Home to Imperial again; with a notice that I will go and *bathe* at Howth;—find D*r.* Evory Kennedy at the door, as I am inquiring about that; go in with him, talk; he carries me in his vehicle to the Howth Station, not possible for this night; *can* do it at Kingstown, drives off for the station *thither*, with repeated invitations that I will dine with him,—finds on the road that Kingstown also will not do, and renews his entreaties to dine, which seeing now no prospect

---

[5] Chief Commissioner of Police.

for the evening, I comply with. K^(y.) drives me all about; streets beautiful, but idle empty; charming little country house (*name* irrecoverable now), beyond some iron-foundry or forge-works, beyond " Rev^(d.) D^(r.) Todd's ", on the Dundrum or Ranelagh side: wife and sisters all out to receive us: sisters, especially elder sister, expected to be charmed at sight of " Thomas Carloil " ! tho' whether they adequately were or not, I cannot say.—Pleasant enough little dinner there; much talk of Pitt Kennedy, a brother now with Napier in India; vivid inventive patriotic man, it would appear, of whose pamphlets they promised me several (since read, not without some real esteem of the headlong Pitt Kennedy) ; other brother is Lord Bath's agent in Monahan,[6]—*hence* chiefly those attentions to me. Ladies gone,—pale, elderly earnest-eyed lean couple of sisters, insipid-beautiful little wife.—" Dr. Cooke Taylor "

[6] Tristram Kennedy, since M.P. for Louth.

is announced, a snuffy, babbling, baddish fellow, whom I had not wished at all specially to see—Strange *dialect* of this man, a Youghal native, London had little altered that; immense lazy gurgling about the throat and palate regions, speech coming out at last not so much in *distinct* pieces and vocables, as in *continuous* condition, semi-masticated speech. A peculiar smile too dwelt on the face of poor snuffy Taylor; I pitied, but could not love him—with his lazy gurgling, semi-masticated, semi-deceitful (and self-deceiving) speech, thought and action. Poor fellow, one of his books that I read " On the Manufacturing regions in 1843 ", was not so bad; Lord Clarendon, a great Patron of his, had got him a pension, brought him over to Ireland :—and now (about a fortnight ago, end of Septr.) I learn that he is dead of cholera, that, better or not so good, I shall never see him again! We drove home together that night, in Dr.

Kennedy's car; I set him out at his house (in some modest clean street, near Merrion Square); two days after, I saw him at the Zoological breakfast; gurgle-snuffle, Cockney-and-Youghal wit again in semi-masticated dialect, with great *expressions* of regard for me, as well as with other half or whole untruths;—and so poor Taylor was to vanish, and the curtains rush down between us impenetrable for evermore. *Allah akbar, Allah Kerim!*

Thursday 5th July.

What people called, what bustle there was of cards and people and appointments and invitations in my little room, I have *quite* forgotten the details of (letters indicate more of it perhaps): what I can remember is mainly what I *did*, and not quite definitely (except with effort) all or the most of that.

Notes and visitors, hospitable messages

and persons, Macdonnel, Col^{l.} Foster, Dr. Kennedy—in real truth I have forgotten *all* the particulars; of Thursday I can remember only a dim hurly-burly, and whirlpool of assiduous hospitable calls and proposals, till about 4 o'clock when a " Sir Philip Crampton,"[7] by no means the most notable of my callers, yet now the most noted in my memory, an aged, rather vain and not very deep-looking Doctor of Physic, came personally to " drive me out,"—drive me to the Phœnix Park and Lord Lieutenant's, as it proved. *Vapid-inane* looking streets in this Dublin, along the quays and everywhere; sad defect of waggons, real *business* vehicles or even gentleman's carriages; nothing but an empty whirl of street cars, huckster carts and other such " trashery." Sir P's. talk, of Twistleton mainly—Phœnix Park, gates, mostly in grass, monument a pyramid, I really don't remember in "admonition" of what,—

[7] Surgeon General.

some victory perhaps? Frazer's Guide-Book would tell. Hay going on, in pikes, coils, perhaps swaths too; patches of potatoes even: a rather dimmish wearisome look. House with wings (at right angles to the body of the building) with esplanade, two sentries, and utter solitude, looked decidedly dull. Sir Ph., some business inside, tho' Ldship. *out*, leaves me till that end; I write my name, with date merely, not with address, in his Lordship's *book* ("haven't the honor to know her Ladyship,") am conducted through empty galleries, into an empty room in the western (or is it *northern?*) wing, am there to wait. Tire soon of waiting; walk off leaving message. Sir P. overtakes me before we reach the gate; sets me down at my Hotel again, after much celebration of his place in the Wicklow Hills, etc., after saluting an elderly roué Prince or Graf something, a very unbeautiful old boiled-looking foreign dignitary (Swede, I think) married to somebody's sister;—and with salutations, takes himself away, muttering about "Zoological Society breakfast on Saturday", and I, barely in time now for Stokes's dinner, behold him no more.

Stokes's dinner was well replenished both with persons and other material, but it proved rather unsuccessful. Foolish Mrs. Stokes, a dim Glasgow lady, with her I made the reverse of progress,—owing chiefly to ill luck. She did bore me to excess, but I did not give way to that; had difficulty however in resisting it; and at length once, when dinner was over, I, answering somebody about something chanced to quote Johnson's, "Did I say anything that *you* understood, Sir?" the poor foolish lady took it to herself; bridled, tossed her head with some kind of indignant-polite ineptitude of a reply; and before long flounced out of the room (with her other ladies, not remembered now), and became, I fear, my enemy for ever! Petrie, a Painter of Landscapes, notable antiquarian, enthusiastic for Brian Boru and all that province of affairs ; an excellent simple, affectionate loveable soul, " dear old Petrie ", he was our chief figure for me: called for *punch* instead of wine, he, and was gradually imitated ; a thin, wrinkly, half-ridiculous, yet mildly dignified man; old bachelor, you could see;[8] speaks with a *panting* manner, difficult to find the word; shews real knowledge, tho' with sad credulity on Irish antiquarian matters ; not knowledge that I saw on anything else. Burton,[9] a young Portrait-Painter; thin-aquiline man, with long thin locks scattered about, with a look of real Painter-talent, but thin, proud-vain; not a pleasant "man of genius." Todd, antiquarian parson (Dean or something), whose house I had seen the night before: little round-faced, dark-complexioned, squat, good humoured and knowing

[8] Mr. Petrie was father of a numerous family.

[9] At present connected with the National Gallery in London.

man; learned in Irish Antiquities he too; not without good instruction on other matters too.—These and a mute or two were the dinner; Stokes, who has a son that carves, sitting at the side; after dinner there came in many other *mutes* who remained such to me. Talk, in spite of my endeavours, took an Irish-versus-English character; wherein, as I really have no respect for Ireland as it now is and has been it was impossible for me to be popular! Good humour in general, tho' not without effort always, did maintain itself. But Stokes, "the son of a United-Irishman" as I heard, grew more and more gloomy, emphatic, contradictory: After 11 I was glad to get away, Petrie and others in kindly mood going with me so far as our roads coincided; and about 12 (I suppose) I got to bed,—and do *not* suppose, also, but *know*, that there was a wretched wakeful night appointed me: some neighbouring guest taken suddenly ill, as I afterwards heard. (I must get on *faster*, be infinitely *briefer* in regard to all this!)

Friday 6th July.

Still in the bath-tub, when my waiter knocked at the door, towards 9; and so soon as let in, gave me a letter with notice that some orderly, or heiduc, or I know not what the term is, was waiting in some vehicle for an answer. Invitation from Lord Clarendon to dine with him on Saturday: here was a nodus! For not having slept, I had resolved to be out of Dublin and the noise without delay; Kennedy had pressed me to his country-house for a dinner on Saturday, and that, tho' not yet in words, I had resolved to do, his hospitality being really urgent and his place quiet;—and now has the Lord Lieutenant come, whose invitation *abolished* by law of etiquette all others! Out of the cold bath, on the spur of the moment, thou shalt decide, and the heiduc waits! Polite answer (well enough really) that I am to quit Dublin that evening, and cannot come. Well so far; so much is tolerably ended. New very polite note came from Lord Clarendon offering me introductions &c. an hour or two after; for which I wrote a 2nd note, "not needed, thousand thanks." This morning I had to breakfast with O'Hagan, where were two young "Fellows of Trinity" great admirers &c. and others to be.

Fellows of Trinity, breakfast and the rest of it accordingly took effect: Talbot Street, —I think they call the place,—lodgings, respectable young barrister's. Hancock the Political-Economy Professor, whom I had seen the day before; he and one Ingram, author of the Repeal Song "True men like you men," were the two Fellows; to whom as a mute brother one Hutton was added, with "invitation to me" from the parental circle, " beautiful place somewhere out near Howth",—very well as it afterwards proved. " Dr. Murray," Theology-Professor of Maynooth, a big burly mass of Catholic Irishism; he and Duffy, with a certain vinaigrous pale shrill logician figure who came in after breakfast, made up the party—Talk again *England versus Ireland;* a sad unreasonable humour pervading all the Irish population on this matter—" England does not hate you at all, nor love you at all; merely values and will pay you according to the work you can do !" No teaching of that unhappy people to understand so much. Dr. Murray, head cropt like stubble, red-skinned face, harsh grey Irish eyes; full of fiery Irish zeal, too, and age, which however he had the art to keep down under buttery-vocables: man of considerable strength, man not to be "loved" by any manner of means! Hancock, and *now* Ingram too, were wholly English (that is to say, Irish-rational) in sentiment. Duffy very *plaintive* with a strain of rage audible in it. Vinaigrous logician, intolerable in that vein, drove me out to smoke. Not a pleasant breakfast in the humour I was then in!

University after, along with these two fellows: Library and busts; Museum, with big dark Curator Ball in it; many knicknacks,—Skull of Swift's Stella, and plaster-cast of Swift: couldn't *write* my name, except all in a tremulous scratchy shiver, in such a state of nerves was I. Todd had, by appointment, been waiting for me; was gone again. Right glad I to get home, and smoke a pipe in peace, till Macdonnel (or somebody) should come for me!—Think it was this day I saw among others Councillor Butt, brought up to me by Duffy: a terrible black burly son of earth: talent visible in him, but still more animalism; big bison-head, black, not *quite* unbrutal: glad when he went off "to the Galway Circuit" or whithersoever.[1]

[1] The late Isaac Butt, M.P.

Sad reflexions upon Dublin, and the animosities that reign in its hungry existence— *Not* now the " Capital " of Ireland ; has Ireland any Capital, or *where* is its future capital to be ? Perhaps Glasgow or Liverpool is its real " capital city " just now ! Here are no longer lords of any kind ; not even the sham-lords with their land-revenues come hither now. The place has no manufactures to speak of ; except of ale and whisky, and a little poplin-work, none that I could hear of. All the " litigation " of Ireland, whatever the wretched Irish people will still pay for the voiding of their quarrels, comes hither ; that and the sham of Government about the Castle and Phœnix Park,—which could as well go anywhither if it were so appointed. Where will the future capital of Ireland be ! Alas, *when* will there any real aristocracy arise (here or elsewhere) to need a Capital for residing in !—

About 4 p m as appointed, Macdonnell

with his car came.² " Son of a United Irishman ", he too. Florid handsome man of 45, with grey hair, keen hazel eyes, not of the *very* best expression: active, quick, intelligent, energetic, with something smelling of the Hypocrite in him, disagreeably limiting all other respect one might willingly pay him. *Talis qualis*, with him through the Streets. Glasnevin tollbar, woman has *not* her groat of change ready; streaks of irregularity, streaks of squalor noticeable in all streets and departments of things. Glasnevin Church; woody, with high enclosures, frail-looking old edifice, roof mainly visible: —at length Glasnevin model-farm—nearly the *best thing*, to appearance, I have yet seen in Ireland. Modest slated buildings, house, school and offices, for real use, and fit for that. Slow-spoken heavy browed schoolmaster croaks out sensible pertinent speech about his affairs: an Ulster man (from

² Sir Alex. MacDonnel.

Larne, I think; name forgotten), has 45 pupils, from 17 to 21 years; they are working about, dibbling, sorting dungheaps, sweeping yards. Mac. speaks to several: coarse rough-haired lads, from all sides of Ireland, intelligent well-doing looks thro' them all. Schooling alternates with this husbandry work. Will become National schoolmasters,—probably factors of estates, if they excel and have luck. Clearly, wherever they go they will be practical missionaries of good order and wise husbandry, these poor lads; *antichaos* missionaries these: good luck go with them, more power to their elbow! Such were my reflexions, expressed partly in some such words. Our heavy-browed croaking-voiced friend has some 30 cows; immense pains to preserve all manure, it is upon this that his husbandry turns. A few pigs, firstrate health in their air. Some 30 acres of ground in all; wholly like a garden for cultivation: best hay, best barley;

best everything. I left him and his rough boys, wishing there were 1,000 such establishments in Ireland : alas, I saw no other in the least equal to it ; doubt if there is another. Mac. talking confidentially and with good insight too of Archbishop Whately &c., set me down at the Hôtel, to meet again at dinner. Hasty enough toilette, then Sir D$^{n.}$ Mc Gregor's close car, and I am whisked out to Drumcondra where the brave Sir D$^{n.}$ himself with wife and son, and a party including Larcom and two ancient Irish Gentlemen &c are waiting.

Pleasant old country-house ; excellent quietly genial and hospitable landlord : dinner pleasant enough really. McDonnell sat by me, somewhat flashy ; Larcom opposite, perhaps do. but it was in the English style. Ancient Irish gentn. were of really excellent breeding, yet Irish altogether : these names quite gone (if ever known, according to the *underbreath* method of introduction),

their figures still perfectly distinct to me.
In white neck cloth, opposite side, a lean
figure of sixty; wrinkly, like a washed
blacksmith in face, yet like a gentn. too,—
elaborately washed and dressed, yet still
dirty-looking; talks of ancient experiences,
in hunting, claret-drinking, experiences of
others his acquaintances, all dead and gone
now, which I have entirely forgotten; high
Irish accent; clean-dirty face wrinkled into
stereotype, of smile or of stoical frown you
couldn't say which: that was one of the
ancient Irishmen; who perhaps had a wife
there? The other, a more florid man with
face not only clean but clean-looking, and
experiences somewhat similar; a truly polite
man in the Irish style: he took me home in
his car. Sir Dn. had handed me a general
missive to the Police Stations "Be service-
able, if you ever can, to this Traveller,"—
which did avail me once. At home lies
Kennedy's letter, enjoining me to *accept* the

Lord Lieutenant's dinner, whither he too is going; which I have already refused! *What* to do to-morrow night? Duffy is to be off to Kilkenny; to lodge with "Dr. Cane the Mayor"; who invites me too (Duffy, on the road to O'Hagan's breakfast, shewed me that), which I accept.

Saturday 7th July.

Wet morning; wait for Kennedy's promised car,—to breakfast in the Zoological gardens. Smoking at the door, buy a newspaper, old hawker pockets my groat, then comes back saying "Yer Hanar has given me by mistake a threepenny!" Old knave, I gave him back his newspaper, ran up stairs for a penny,—discover that the threepenny has a hole drilled in it, that it is his,—and that I am done! He is off when I come down—Petrie under an umbrella, but no

Kennedy still. We call a car, we two; I give him my "Note to Chambers Walker, Barrister," whom he knows, who will take me up at Sligo, when he (P) will join us, and we shall be happy. Well;—we shall see. Muddy Street, rain about done; carboy coming over one of the bridges, drives against the side of our car, seemed to me to see clearly for some instants that he *must* do such a thing, but to feel all the while that it would be so convenient to him *if* he didn't,—a reckless humour, *ignoring* of the inevitable, which I saw often enough in Ireland. Even the mild Petrie swore, and brandished his umbrella. "How could I help it?; could I stop, and I goin' so rapid!" At the gate of Zoological which is in Phoenix Park, were Hancock, Ball of the Museum, another Ball of the Poor-law,[3] Cooke Taylor (for the last time, poor soul!), and others strolling under

[3] Mr. John Ball, since M.P. and President of the Alpine Club.

the wet boscage : breakfast now got served in a dim very damp kind of place (like some small rotunda, for limited public-meetings),— unpleasant enough wholly; and we got out into the gardens, and walked smoking, with freer talk (of mine mainly) good for little. Animals &c.,—Public subscription scanty— Government helps :—adieu to it. In Kennedy's car to Sackville Street; Poor law Ball and a whole set of us; pause at Sackville street, part go on, part will take me to Royal Irish Academy, after I have got my letters of this morning's post. With Hancock I settle that *Hutton* this night shall lodge me at Howth; that he and Ingram shall escort me out thither, when I will bathe. Nerves and health—ach Gott, be *silent* of them!

Royal Irish Academy really has an interesting Museum : Petrie does the honours with enthusiasm. Big old iron cross (smith's name on it in Irish, and date about 1100 or so, ingenious old smith really); Second Book of Clogher (tremendously old, said Petrie), torques, copper razor, porridge-pots, bog butter (tastes like wax), bog-cheese (didn't taste that, or even see); stone mallets (with cattle-bones copious where they are found,— "old savage feasting-places"): really an interesting Museum, for everything has a certain *authenticity*, as well as national or other significance, too often wanting in such places. Next to Petrie, my most assiduous expositor was the Secy., whom I had seen at Stokes's; a mute, but who spoke now and civilly and to the purpose. Bustle-bustle. Evory Kennedy and others making up a route for me in the library room: at length, in a kind of paroxysm, I bid adieu to them all, and get away,—to the Hotel to pack and settle.

Larcom next comes: for an hour and half in Board of Works with him. Sir W. Petty's *old* survey of Irish lands (in another office from L's); Larcom's new one,—very ingenious; coloured map, with dots, figures referring you to tables, where is a complete account of all estates, with their pauperisms, liabilities, rents, resources: for behoof of the Poor law Commrs. and their " electoral divisions"; a really meritorious and as I fancy most valuable work. Kirwan a western squire accidentally there; astonished at me, poor fellow, but does not hate me, invites me even. Larcom to Hotel door with me: adieu, adieu! to the Hotel people too, who have done all things zealously for me, and even schemed me out a route for the morrow (*wrong*, as it proved, alas!) I bid affecting adieus; and Ingram and Hancock bowl me off to the Howth Railway. Second-class, say they, but gentn. tho' crowded: Dublin cockneys on a Saturday.

The Hutton house, that evening amid "Socinian" really well-conditioned people: much should not be said of it. Hospitality's self: tall silent-looking Father Hutton (for they live at Ballydoyle, this side of Howth) meets me with " hopes" &c. at the Station there : car is to follow us to Howth, where I am to bathe, whither we now roll on. Bathe, bad bathing-ground, tide being out, wound heel in the stones (slippers *were* in the Bathing Machine, but people *didn't tell me*); *Cornish* Pilchard-sloops fishing here; dirty village; big old Abbey over-grown with thistles, nettles, burdocks and the extremity of squalor, to which we get access thro' dark cabins by the *back windows*,—leaving a few coppers amid hallelujahs of thanks. Car, get wrapped, and drive to Lord Howth's gate: admittance there, to those of us on foot, not without difficulty : beautiful avenue, beautiful still house looking out over the still sea at eventide; among the beautifullest places I ever saw. Lord Howth a *racer*, away now, with all his turf-equipments; *Cornish* people obliged to come and fish his Bay,—his mainly for 500 years back, I believe.

Call in for a Cousin Hutton (poor George Darley's class-fellow, a barrister, I afterwards find) who is to go with us; twilight getting darker and darker,—I still without dinner, and growing cold, reduced to tobacco merely! Arrive at last; succedaneum for dinner is readily provided, consumed along with coffee; night passes, not intolerably, tho' silence for me was none; alas, on reflecting, I had not come there for silence! Cousin Hutton and Ingram off; a clever indignant kind of little fellow the latter. Mrs Hutton, big black eyes *struggling* to be in earnest; four young ladies sewing,—*schöne kinder* truly.—At last do get to bed; sleep sound till 6, bemoaned by the everlasting main. "No train (Sunday) at the hour given by Imperial Hotel people," so it appears! The good Huttons have decided to send me by their carriage. Excellent people; poor little streetkin of Ballydoyle fronting a wide waste of sea-sands (fisher people, I suppose): peace and good be with you!

Sunday 8th July.

Escorted by Hancock and young Hutton am set down at Imperial Hotel, and thence my assiduous Familiar brings out luggage, in a car to Kildare Railway Station, (in the extreme west,—King's or Temple-bridge, do they call it?): three quarters of an hour too soon; rather wearisome the waiting. Fields all about have a weedy look, ditches rather dirty; houses in view, extensive some of them, have a patched dilapidated air—lime-pointing on *roofs* (as I gradually found) is uncommonly frequent in Ireland; d$^{o.}$ white-washing to cover a multitude of sins: grey time-worn look in consequence—lime is every-where abundant in Ireland; few bogs them-selves but are close in the neighbourhood of lime.

Start at last: second class but *not* quite

Gent^n· this time; plenty of *room* however. Irish traveller alone in my compartment; big *horse*-faced elderly; not a bad fellow (a Wexforder?),—for Limerick I suppose. Two Irish *gents* (if not gent^n·) in the next compartment (for we were all visible to one another); mixed rusticity or cockneyity, not remembered, in the other. Gents had both of them their tickets stuck in hatband; good, and often seen since in Scotland and elsewhere: talked to one another, loud but empty: first gent beaming black animal eyes, florid, ostentatious, voracious-looking: a sensual gent; neighbour had his back towards me, and he is lost: both went out awhile before me. —Kildare Station between 12 and 1 (I think): indifferent *porterage*—Country with hay and crops, in spite of occasional bogs, had been good,—waving champaign with Wicklow Hills in the distance; railway well enough, tho' sometimes at stations or the like some little thing was wrong.—Letter of the Inscription knocked off, or the like. This then is Kildare :—but alas I nowhere see the city; above all, see no Peter Fitzgerald, whom I expected here to receive me. In the open space, which lies behind the station, get a view of Kildare, round tower, black and high, with old ruin of cathedral, on a height half a mile off; poor enough "City" to all appearance! Ask for St. Bridget's "Fire Tower-house" that once was; nobody knows it; one young fellow pretends (and only pretends I think) to know it. Two gentlemen, fat fellows, out of the train seemingly had seen the label on my luggage; rush round to ask me eagerly, "Are you Mr. Thomas Carloil?" I thought they had been Fitzgerald, and joyfully answered and enquired: alas, no they were Mr. Something else altogether, and had to roll away again next instant. Seeing no Fitzgerald I had to bargain with a car-man (I think there was but one), and roll away towards Halverstown—up a steepish narrow road to Kildare first.

Kildare, as I entered it looked worse and worse : one of the wretchedest wild villages I ever saw ; and full of ragged beggars this day (Sunday),—exotic altogether, "like a village in Dahomey," man and Church both. Knots of worshipping people hung about the streets, and every-where round them hovered a harpy-swarm of clamorous mendicants, men, women, children :—a village *winged,* as if a flight of harpies had alighted in it ! In Dublin I had seen winged groups, but not *much* worse than some Irish groups in London that year : here for the first time was "Irish beggary" itself ! —From the centre or top of the village I was speeding thro', where the Cathedral and Round Tower disclose, or properly had disclosed, themselves on my right, I turn a little to survey them; and here Fitzgerald and lady, hospitable pair, turn up and make themselves known to me. *A la bonne heure!*

Beggars, beggars; walk through the wretched streets, Nunneries here, big chapel here, my hosts are Catholics: I wait smoking in their carriage till they make a call; won't give beggars anything who depart, all but 2, young fellows, cowering nearly naked on opposite sides of me 20 yards off. "Take this groat and divide it between you!" Explosion of thanks; exeunt round the corner: re-enter one: "Ach, yer honor! He won't give me the two pence"—"Then why don't you lick him, you blockhead, till he either die or give it you?" Two citizens, within hearing, burst into a laugh.—Home to Halverstown, pleasant rough-cultivated country, ragged hedges, fertile weedy fields, one *good* farmstead or two: Mrs. Purcell welcomes us with genial smiles.

Monday 9th July.

9 July 1849. Went from Halverstown to

Glendalough, wonderful passage, especially after Holywood a desolate hamlet among the hills. Scarecrow figures all busy among their peats, ragged all, old straw hats, old grey loose coats in tatters, vernacular aspect all. Horse unwilling to perform uphill, at length downhill too; we mostly walk. Young shepherd, very young gossoon (had been herding with somebody for no wages), was now sent home to " the Churches," where he had a brother (minor) and sister left,—fibbed to me (as I found in the begging line), otherwise good and pitiable. I made him mount downhill. Resemblance to Galloway, in the hills, or to the pass beyond Dalveen; hills *all* black and boggy, some very craggy too; cattle kyloes, sheep mongrels: wild stony huts, patches of corn few yards in area. [Woman near Kilcullen milking a goat in the morning—goats frequent enough here, pick living in the ditches]. Wicklow Gap; Lead Mines; stone on the road. Guide (a sulky stupid creature) drives over it eyes open.—Like much here, like potatoe-culture. Cottages mostly cabins to the right hand under the road, and more frequent all the way down. Some mine-works (water wheel *going*), many mine shafts all the way down. At bottom inn, shop, swift river, steps, beggars, churches, churchyard, wreck of *grey* antiquity grown *black;* round tower— "Cathedral," small Church with arch roof still entire, and little round belfry (? windows in it) at one end. Third church there; then lower and upper lake opening. Strait cul-de-sac of a glen, a spoke (or radius) making an *angle* with Wicklow Gap Glen : fit *pot* among the black mountains for St Kevin to macerate himself in. Scarecrow boatman; big mouth, rags, hunger and good humour, has his "chance" (of this best with strangers) by way of wages. Woman squirrel clambering on the rocks to shew St Kevin's Bed; which needed no "shewing" at all; husband had deserted her, children all dead in workhouse but one; shed under a cliff; food as the ravens. New carman, rapid, good-humoured and loquacious; miner hurt among the hills; man galloping for doctor and priest; howl of woman's lamentation heard among the twilight mountains; very miserable to hear. No whiskey at Trainer's; handsome gift of milk by pretty daughter, brought sixpence all the same. Home about 10; expense enormous, 30/. or more, to *me*.

Tuesday 10 July.

Tuesday 10th July. Love, the Scotch farmer; excellent farming. Gent^n (Burrowes) that wouldn't allow draining; 800 people *took* the Common; priest had petitioned Peel 10 years ago, but took no notice; peasant vagrants did, and here their cabins and grottos all *are*. Fitz's brother (a useful good servant) has a cabin and field there, with wife in it; good ground if it were drained. All Commons have been settled that way; once they were put away from, and the ditches levelled *twice* (so said our first carman, a fine active lad) the *third* time it held, and so they stay. O'Connor (Mrs Purcell's brother) a smart dandyish landlord, complained dreadfully of these " Commoners" now mostly *paupers;* nobody's property once, now *his* (to fen). All creatures, Love among the rest, cling to the potatoe, as the one hope or possibility they have or ever dream of; look upon the chance of failure, as our Sulky did upon the stone "perhaps I'll get over it." In the afternoon Curragh of Kildare, best of race courses, a sea of beautiful green land, with fine cropt furze on it here and there, a fine race-stand (like the best parish church) at one end, saddling house &$^c\cdot$; racing apparatus enough; and *work* for about 10,000 people if they were set to it instead of left to beg, (circle of 3 miles, 4,000 acres, look?)

Newbridge village and big barrack; Liffey both at Kilcullen and it; *Monastery*, Mrs P. saluted priest; people all lounging, village idle, silent, many houses *down*.—Railway, whirl of dust, smoke and screaming uproar, past Kildare again, past Athy (*A-thigh*) old walls, now a village, Wexford hills on this hand, Q's County hills on that: good green wavy country alternating with detestable bogs to Carlow—saw into the grey old hungry-looking stones as we whirled past in the evening sun—Railway Station, broken windows there (done by mischievous boys), letters knocked off &c., now and then all the way from Dublin. Car at Bagnalstown, eloquent beggar. "More power to you "wherever you go! The Lord Almighty "preserve your honor from all sickness and "hurt and the dangers of the year!" &c. &c. Never saw such begging in this world; often get into a rage at it. On to Kilkenny (over the Barrow &c.); noisy vulgar fellow, talks, seems to know me. Castle Inn door; Dr Cane's where I now am [writing in dressing gown] 7 a.m., not having slept; morning the flower of summer; town old decayed and grey.

Addenda (7 Oct^r·) to the two foregoing entries.—Hideous crowds of beggars at Glendalough—offering guideship &^c·. No guide needed. Little black-eyed boy, *beautiful* orphan beggar, forces himself on us at last; ditto grey-eyed little girl, with fish her uncle had caught. Scarecrow boatman, his clothes or rags hung on him like *tapestry*, when the wind blew he expanded like a tulip: *first* of many such conditions of dress. "King O'Toole's tomb". "Tim Byrne" (Burn they pronounced), spoken to, he, the one whole-coated farmer of the place; many *Byrnes* hereabouts. Could not make out the meaning or origin of Glendalough; at last found S^t· Kevin (natural in S^t· K) to be the *central* fact: the "Kings" O'Toole, O'Byrne &^c· &^c· had dedicated chapels to him, bequeathing their own bodies to be buried there, as unspeakably advantageous for them; straight road to Heaven for them perhaps. Many burials *still* here; tombstones, all of mica-slate, slice off into obliteration within the century. One arch (there still remains another) of entrance to " Cathedral " had fallen *last* year (or year before?) Fount, and miracles in "Patron-time"; "Patterun" is Kevin himself; " St. Kevin's be your bed! " Brought heath and ivy from Glendalough; grimmest spot in my memory.

Halvertstown a quiet original little country-seat; beautiful in the summer greenness, and all wearing an exotic look; "*Irish Mæcænas*" kind of air. Purcell, a notable Irishman, had run coaches, made a *farm* often at his coach station; this was one. Mass-chapel in it (priest *didn't* appear); galleries, summer hall; dining room lighted with glass dome; number of tolerable pictures;—place added to gradually; very good;

my room excellent. Greenhouse, pretty shrubbery with "big stone" in it (Ed$^{d.}$ Fitz$^{d's.}$); trees round, children had a little coach with *goats* harnessed: *good* order reigning (or strenuously attempting to reign) everywhere. —Kilcullen (near by) has a Round Tower: height where the rebels of '98 had a skirmish. Lord Waterford's shooting-lodge, at "Trainers" (on the road to Glendalough), miserable bare place. Remember something of Kilcullen town itself: through which the kind M$^{rs.}$ Purcell drove me, that afternoon, as well as over Curragh &$^c.$ to Station at Kildare.

Kildare Railway; big blockhead, sitting with his dirty feet on seat opposite, not stirring them for me, who wanted to sit there: "One thing we're all agreed on," said he "we're very *ill governed;* Whig, Tory, Radical, Repealer, all admit we're very ill governed!"—I thought to myself "Yes indeed: you govern yourself. He that would govern you well, would probably surprise you much my friend,—laying a hearty horsewhip over that back of your's." "*No smoking allowed*"; passengers had erased the " No." Coarse young man entering, took out his pipe, and smoked without apology. Second Class; went no more in *that*—Carlow, " Hungry Street:" remember it still well, and the few human figures stalking about in it: red, dusty-looking evening, to *us* (in rail) dusty and windy. Of Bagnalstown, saw nothing but Station, (Railway is still in progress), and some streak of distant housetops, behind (westward) of that; and one little inn at the extremity where our car halted and the beggars were. Dusty, dusky evening to Kilkenny. Lord Clifden's property; racer, has a horse called " Justice to Ireland" (said my vulgar friend);—Kilkenny long feeble street of suburb; sinks *hollow* near the Castle; bridge and river there; then rapidly up is inn. Car to D[r] Cane's after delay: O'Shaugnessy and the other two poor-law Inspectors at dinner there: still waiting (8½ or 9 p m), Duffy, Cane, and M^rs. C.; warm welcome: queer old house; my *foot* a little sprained (from Halvertstown and Love's potatoe-field—didn't trouble me above another day), D^r C bandaged it,—but my *tay* was very cold and bad. Talking difficult; no good of the O'Shaughnessys, no good of anything till I got away to bed. [*End of addenda.*]

Wednesday 11*th July.*

Wake early, sound of jackdaws, curious old room, two windows to street, one behind; tops of all come down (*not* bottoms up, of all); plentiful thorough draft: look out over the grey old dilapidated town: smoke; to bed again, but sleep returns not. O'Shaughnessy (after letters written &^c.) takes us out in Cane's carriage to look over his poor-houses.—Had seen the "Market-morning" before; crowd of people under the pillars, eggs, lean fowls and other small-trash.—Coblers 3 or 4 working on the street.—Letter *to* Jane (to Mother next day.—Still here),—on a very *curious* kind of "table" (a hydrasting cylinder in fact), the only one I had convenient! O'Shaughnessy's subsidiary poor-house (old brewhouse, I think), workhouse being filled to bursting: with some 8,000 (?) paupers in *all*. Many women here; carding cotton, knitting, spinning &c. &c. place and they very clean;—"but one *can*," bad enough! In other Irish workhouses, saw the like; but nowhere ever *so* well. Big Church or Cathedral, of blue stones, *limestony* in appearance, a-building near this spot. Buttermilk pails (in this subsidiary poor-house, as in *all* over Ireland)—tasted from one; not bad on hot day. Eheu!—*omitted* other subsidiary poor-houses (I think); walked towards original *workhouse* with its 3,000:

—towards Cathedral, round tower &c. *first;* detestable *lagoon* evaporating, with houses and dusty streets round it; can't get at it to drain! Round tower has wooden ladder to top; sit there, very high, view hungry-looking, parched, bare, Sahara-looking. Cathedral closes, empty, silent, and welcome; Cathedral seen as *duty;* Old *Council House* (of Kilkenny Council in 1642)[1] omitted by oversight; in Cathedral, some monuments not memorable to me; one (of 1649 time) a Councillor's had been *erased.* Day dreadfully hot; get away to workhouse, where Duffy leaves me.

Workhouse; huge chaos, *ordered* " as one could;"—O'S., poor light little *Corker* (he is from Cork, and a really active creature), proved to be the *best* of all the "orderers," I saw in Ireland in this office; but his establishment, the first I had ever seen, quite shocked me. Huge arrangements for eating,

[1] Meeting-place of the Confederation of Kilkenny.

baking, stacks of Indian meal stirabout; 1000 or 2000 great hulks of men lying piled up within brick walls, in such a country, in such a day! Did a *greater* violence to the law of nature ever before present itself to sight, if one *had* an eye to *see* it? Schools, for girls, rather goodish; for boys, clearly bad; forward, impudent *routine*—scholar, one boy, with strong Irish physiognomy,—getting bred to be an impudent superficial pretender. So; or else sit altogether stagnant, and so far as you can, *rot*. Hospital: haggard ghastliness of some looks,—literally, their eyes grown " colorless " (as Mahomet describes the horror of the Day of Judgment) ; "take me home!" one half-mad was urging; a deaf-man ; ghastly *flattery* of us by another, (*his* were the eyes): ah me! boys drilling, men still piled within their walls: no hope but of stirabout; swine's meat, swine's *destiny* (I gradually saw): right glad to get *away*. Idle people, on road to castle; sitting on street curbstones, &c.; numerous in the summer afternoon; idle old city; can't well think how they live. Castle "superb" enough but no heart for it; no portraits that I care about,—not even a *certain* likeness of the Duke James, the *Great* of Ormond; *pay* my half-crown; won't write in the album;—home dead-tired; and O'S. is to come and dine. Of dinner little rememberable at all. Strange dialect of M^{rs.} Dr. Cane, a Wicklow lady,—made a canvas case for my writing case this day, good hostess! came of Scotch people; rings with such a *lilt* in speaking as is unexampled hitherto; all is *i's*, *oi's*, &c.;—excellent mother and wife, so far as heart goes, "sure-ly." Snuffy editors, low-bred but not without energy, *once* "all for repale," now out of that;—have little or no memory of what they said or did. Dr. Cane himself, lately in prison for "repale," now free and Mayor again, is really a person of superior worth. Tall, straight, heavy man, with grey eyes and smallish globular black head; deep bass voice, with which he speaks slowly, solemnly, as if he were preaching. Irish (moral) Grandison—touch of that in him; sympathy with all that is good and manly however, and continual effort towards that. Likes me, is hospitably kind to me, and I am grateful to him. Up stairs about 8 o'clock (to smoke, I think), lie down on rough ottoman at bed's end, for 5 minutes; —fall dead asleep, and Duffy wakes me at one o'clock! We are to go to-morrow morning towards Waterford—I slept again, till towards six, and then wrote to my mother, as well as looked into "Commercial Reading rooms" &c. opposite me in the ancient narrow street. Jackdaws and lime-pointed old slate roofs were my prospect otherwise fore and aft. Crown of the year now in regard to *heat*.

Thursday 12th *July.*

Other stranger (snuffy editor *now?*) to breakfast, admires Gray's Scheme,—Edin. Gray, a projector of *money* schemes—to give all the world *money* at will, " do nicely for Ireland, indeed " thought I or said. Off with Duffy, in Dr.'s chariot, to Railway Station about 10½ a.m. First Class rail: silent, excellent; ends at Thomastown in about an hour. Private car there; shady little street, hot, close, little inn, while they are packing luggage. Towards Waterford, railway men *again* breaking ground, groups of them visible twice.—Rawboned peasant spoken to, striding with us up a hill; sadly off since potatoes went and evictions came; struggling to do better. Jerpoint Abbey, huge *distressing* mass of ruins, huts leaning on the back of it,—to me nothing worth at all; or less than nothing of *dilettantism* must join with it.

Rest of the road singularly *forgotten*; Duffy keeping me so busy at *talk* I suppose! Squalid hamlets, ditto cottages by the wayside, with their lean goats and vermin, I have forgotten the details of them; at present they (try to) re-emerge big and vague,— dim, worthless. " Ballyhack; " but I suppose it was " Mullinavat " where our man drew up; tried for buttermilk, at the little idle shop in the little idle village,—unattainable. " Carrickshock " farm on the *west*, fronting us (hedges or bushey ground about a mile off), where " 18 police," seizing for tithes, were set upon and all killed some 18 or more years ago. And next? Vacancy, not even our talk remembered in the least;—probably of questions which I had to answer. Duffy *hummed* continually, with words but without tune, whenever I ceased speaking; my own mood was one of silent stony uneasiness. *Saw* the Suir coming? my face was to the west; suppose we must have gone by " the new road from Mullinavat;" remember, partly *broken* (Duffy hoped from "repale insurrection," alas it was from bad masonry); the road too was broad and not very hilly;— at length under steep cliffs we come to the end of Waterford long wooden bridge; rattle over to the bright trim-looking long quay with its high substantial row of houses on the other side, rattle along the same, and at last are shoved out, very dusty and dim, at Commercial Hotel, where it, not far from ending, is intersected by a broad street at right angles; street as I afterwards found, where "Meagher" (the now convict) lived, and where his father still lives. (Mem. On the Friday morning at Dublin I had seen a big flaring lithograph portrait (whose I didn't know, like *Lockhart* somewhat) with the people murmuring sympathy over it, in a shop window near the end of Sackville Street: it was now removed; must have been M.'s)—*This* (Thursday) afternoon, was it now that I argued with Duffy about Smith O'Brien; I infinitely vilipending, he hotly eulogizing the said Smith?

At Waterford it was Assize time and the C$^{l.}$ Hotel was rather in an encumbered state: two small bed-rooms, without fireplaces, in third floor; mine looks out seaward, over clean courts, house roofs, and I think sees a bit of country, perhaps even of sea. Letters; one from Lord Stuart de Decies, (volunteer thro' poor-law Ball), to whom I write that I *will* come, and enclosing Lord Monteagle's letter. At dinner (*excellent* sole, raises question of London soles, *they* are Waterford fish but deteriorated by the transfer). L$^{d.}$ Carew's servant is here, Mr. Currey, Duke of Devonshire's agent from Lismore is here; send my letters to them. Brief interview with L$^{d.}$ Carew & son on the morrow here, nothing more; much negociation with Mr. Currey, eager to do the honours to me, in which enterprise he persisted and succeeded. Agent, kind of trading man, to whom I had a letter from the Fitzgeralds: not at home; leave it. Man comes after 10, talks civilly, lamentingly; send him off. A Quaker, one of Todhunter's list, Strangman I think, after much enquiry, " doesn't now live in town." (Quaker Todhunter of Dublin had, by Dr Kennedy's request, sent me to Kilkenny a list of Quakers in all the principal towns—did see one of them at Limerick). Duffy's Father Something was also not at home: so we returned to the hotel for tea.—Father Someother-thing, a silly, fluctuating free-spoken priest, joined us in that meal; we to breakfast with him to morrow.—Smoke cigar along the quay.—the southernmost part of it beyond our Hôtel; talk with shopkeeper kind of man there, leaning over the balustrade, looking at the few ships and boats; Waterford's Commerce ruined,—this was the sum of *all* my enquiries,—2,000 hands acquainted with curing bacon had left the place, bacon (owing to potatoe failure) having ended. Butter d°., Cattle d°; all has ended "for the time". Good many warehouses, *three* in one place on the quay you may now see shut.—Walk *late* up to the Post Office : big watchman, with grappling hook for drunk men, patrolling the Dock quay;—" accidents may happen, sir !" Wretched state of *my* poor clay carcase at that time ; Currey has had a message for me; talk with him, hour and more, after my return ; young smart clever-looking man ; of lawyer and wholly English dialect and aspect: *won't* let me pass without *his* hospitalities tho' now I need them not. Bed at last, but no great shakes of a sleep.

Friday 13th July.

Breakfast with the Father Something; steepish street far back in the City; other younger Father with him;—clever man this, black-eyed florid man of thirty this, not ill informed, and appears to have an element of real zeal in him, which is rare among these people. Priest's breakfast and equipment nothing special; that of a poor schoolmaster or the like, living in lodgings with a rude old woman and her niece or daughter: talk also similar,—putting Irish for Scotch, the thing already known to me. —To see some Charitable Catholic Schools; far off, day hot, I getting ill: Irish monk (pallid, tall, dull-looking Irishman of 50) takes us hospitably; 40 or 50 boys, all Catholic, with good apparatus—these he silently *won't* set agoing for us ("holiday" or some such thing); we have to *look* at them with what approval we can. To the hotel, I with younger priest; totally sick and miserable when I arrive, take refuge up stairs on three chairs, and there lie, obstinate to speak to no man till our car go off. Currey does see me however; *settles* at last,—will do the impossible (tho' unnecessary), and not be satisfied without doing it. Car at last (after L$^{d.}$ Carew &^{c}); in the hot afternoon still high we rattle forth into the dust.

Dust, dust, wind is arear of us (or some *dusty* way it blows) on the car; and there is no comfort but patience, distant *view* of green, and occasionally a cigar. The wind, dusty or not, refreshes, considerably cures my sick nerves, as it always does. Strait dusty places: goats chained together with straw-rope; " repale would be agreeable ! " Scrubby ill-cultivated country; Duffy talking much, that is, making me talk. Hedges mostly of *gorse*, not one of them will turn any kind of cattle,—alas I found that the universal rule in Ireland, not one fence in 500 that will *turn*. Gorse they are almost all, and *without* attention paid : emblematic enough. Kilmacthomas, clear white village hanging on the steep declivity. Duffy discovered; enthusiasm of all for him, even the (Galway) policeman. Driver privately whispers me " he would like to give a cheer for that gent."— " Don't, it would do him no good." Other policeman *drunk*, not mischievous but babbling-drunk; didn't see another in that or any such condition in all my travels. We were in the lower *end* of Kilmacthomas; upwards it *climbed* the brae, to the rightward, with most decisive steepness: a poor small place, with houses or huts all limewashed, street torn up by rain-streams; lives very, bright with me yet, as seen in the bright summer afternoon. Off again; towards Dungarvan; the sun veiled from us, the wind rising when we arrive there, about 5 or 6 o'clock. "Shake Dungarvan,"[5] an Irish proverb, means to make a splutter, or loud demonstration of any kind. Embanked road by way of approach,—mud of lagoon on each side, lefthand is sea-ward as you enter;—very

[5] "Make Dungarvan shake."

bleak and windy just now. Car is shifted; populace all out gazing at Duffy, as if they would have stared thro' and thro' him;—would I were at Dromana for one; at Cappoquin first. This is a poor one-horse car; and our accommodation is not superb. Duffy and I on the south side; had been on the north before. N.B. Absurd report about Shiel M.P. before we reached Dungarvan; ("£3,000,000 short in the Mint, somebody's robbery;" Duffy had heard it as a truth at Waterford too, and our driver was full of it); *meeting* of the two brother cars and loud banter of the drivers. These things, too, if they had any worth when recollected, I recollect. Cappoquin at last, in the thickening dusk, 8½ I suppose; leave Duffy at the Inn, and get a car for Dromana, in a most dusty, stiffened, petrified, far from enviable condition. Dromana drawbridge—(over some river tributary of the Blackwater), Dromana park, huge square grey house and deep solitude;

am admitted, received with real hospitality and a beautiful quiet politeness (tho' my Waterford letter *has* not been received); and, once entirely stript, washed, and otherwise refreshed, commit myself to the new kindly element, pure element that surrounds me. Sleep,—O the beautiful big old English bed !, and bedroom big as ballroom, looking out on woody precipices that overhang the Blackwater. Begirt with mere silence! I slept and again slept, a heavy sleep; still remembered with thankfulness.

Saturday 14th July.

Beautiful breezy sunny morning; wide waving wooded lawn, new cropt of *hay;* huge square old grey mansion hanging on the woody brow or (Drom, *Drum*) over the river with steps, paths &c cut in the steep;— grand silence everywhere, huge *empty* hall like a Cathedral when you entered;—all the family away but Ld Stuart and a stepdaughter Baroness, semi-german, and married to a German now fighting against the Hungarians (Baroness *zealous* for him). The pleasantest morning and day of all my Tour. —Quiet simple breakfast; all in excellent *order* (tea *hot* &^c as you find it rarely in a great house); my letter comes *now* and we have a nice quiet hour or two, we three, over this and other things; ride with Lord Stuart to gardens, thro' woods to village of Dromana; clean slated hamlet with church; founded by predecessor (70 or 80 years ago) for *weaving*. Ulster weavers have all *ceased* here; posterity lives by country labour, reasonably well, you would say. This was the limit of our ride. All trim, rational, well ordered here; Ld Stuart himself good, quite English in style, and with the good-natured candid-*drawling*-dialect (*à la* Twistleton) that reminds you of England. Talent enough too, and a sensibility to fun among other things; man of fifty, smallish black eyes, full cheeks, expression of patience with *capability* of action, with the most perfect politeness at all points. Will drive me to Mount Melleray " Monastery ;" does so; off about one. Other side of Cappoquin; road wilder, mounting towards Knockmeildown mountains, which had made figure last night, which make a great figure, among the other fine objects, from Dromana Park; arrive at Melleray in an hour or so.

Hooded monks ;—actually in brown coarse woollen sacks, that reach to the knee, with funnel shaped hood that can be thrown back; Irish physiognomy in a new guize! Labourers working in the field at hay &c; *Country* people they, I observe, *presided* over by a monk.—Entrance, squalid hordes of beggars sit waiting; Irish *accent* from beneath the hood, as a " brother" admits us; learning the Lordship's *quality* he hastens off for " the prior": a tallish, lean, not very prepossessing Irishman of 40, who conducts us thenceforth. Banished from Mount Meilleraye in France about 1830 for quasi-political reasons; the first of these Irishmen arrive penniless at Cork, know not what to do : a protestant Sir Something gives them " waste land," wild craggy moor on this upland of the Knockmeildowns, charitable Catholics intervene, with other help : they struggle, prosper, and are now as we see. Good bit of ground *cleared*, drained, and productive; more in clear progress thereto, big simple square of buildings &c (*Chapel* very grand, done by monks all the decorations), dormitory very large, wholly wooden and clean : bakehouse, poor library, nasty *tubs* of cold stirabout (coarsest I ever saw) for beggars; silence; each monk, when bidden do anything, does it, folds hands over breast, and disappears with a *large* smile and a low bow ;—curious enough to look upon indeed ! Garden rather weedy, a few monks poking about in it; work rather make-believe I feared; offices in the rear; extensive peat-stack, mill; *body* of haymakers, one or two young monks actually *making* hay. Rise at 2 a.m. to their devotions; have really to go thro' a great deal of drill-exercise thro' the day, independently of work. One poor fellow in the library has been dabbling a bit in the elements of geometry,— elemental yet ingenious. "The other night lead spout has been torn off from our cow-house there; new thing theft from *us*."— Excellent brown bread, milk and butter, is offered for viaticum; Lord Stuart, I see, smuggles some gift of money; and with blessings we are rolled away again. The new "Monastery" must have accumulated several 1000 pounds of *property* in these 17 or more or fewer years, in spite of its continual charities to beggars; but this itself, I take it must be very much the result of public *Charity* (Catholic Ireland much approving of them); and I confess the whole business had, lurking under it for me, at this year of grace, a certain *dramatic* character, as if they were " doing it." Inevitable at this year of grace, I fear! Hard work I didn't see monks doing : except it were one young fellow who was actually forking hay; food, glory, dim notion of getting to Heaven, too, I suppose these are motive enough for a man of average Irish insight? The saddest fact I heard about these poor monks was, that the Prior had discovered some of them surveying the Youghal-and-Cappoquin steamer, watching its arrival, from their high moor as the event of *their* day ; and had reprovingly taken away their telescope : ah me !—potatoe failure had sadly marred *them* too; they had sold their fine organ (a pious gift) lately, and even, as I heard, their " whole stock of poultry " in the famine year.

One Sir — Shaw, fine Ayrshire man, an old Peninsula soldier, Lord S's agent here, to dinner with us; fine hearty hoary old soldier, rattles pleasantly away: " Napier used to say, if you would be a soldier learn to *sleep!*" Few can do it: Napoleon could. Snatch sleep whenever and wherever there is a chance. About 10 I had to tear myself up, and with real pathos snatch myself away from these excellent people; their car waits for me, in the dim summer night, an *English* driver: and thro' Cappoquin I am hurried to Lismore, smoking, and looking into the dark boscage, into the dark world.—Bridge building at Cappoquin, old bridge at Lismore Castle, steepish ascent, old gatehouse, passage, silent court; and at one of the corners (left hand, or river, side), Currey having done the impossible, *posted,* namely, in bespoken relays of cars all the way from Waterford, is here some minutes ago to receive me; Duke of Devonshire's impulse,—strange enough,—on *me.* Across the court, or through long silent passages to an excellent room and bed, fitted up as for persons of quality; and there, bemurmured by the Blackwater, quite happy had I not been so dyspeptic incurable a creature, I once more dissolve in grateful sleep under the clouds and stars.

Sunday 15th July.

Bright sunny morning again; day too hot; and I, alas, internally too hot. Noble old Castle, all sumptuous, clean, dry, and utterly vacant (only a poor Irish housekeeper, old, lame, clean, loitering on the stairs, with an appetite for shillings),—all mine for a few hours; like a palace of the fairies. Drive towards the mountains; to a school-house, to be developed into *Agricultural* school by "the Duke": Currey, kind active man, having his gig ready. Duke's property *ends* at the very peak of the very highest Knockmeildown, a cone that had been conspicuous to me these two days; well shaded country, up the clearest of little rivers; schoolhouse atop, very windy; two girls alone in the house.—Currey salutes the people in Irish (which he has learned) as we drive down again; meet many "coming from chapel" or hanging about the road; a certain "squire" Something is in talk with certain common people, nods to C^y, we turn to the right when near Lismore; get into the Park of some *anarchic* squire (has been shot at, I think); bars and obstacles, high plantations *dying* for long want of the axe; ugliest of houses, with its back to us, or ugly posterior to us; anarchy reigns *within* (I am told) as without. Down at last towards Blackwater side; where C$^{s\cdot}$ messenger, that was to row us, slightly *fails;* Currey, leaving horse, leaving message with somebody on the road, takes me thro' the fat rough meadows; gets into the boat, rows me himself (good man), I steering; fat rough meadows, scraggy border of trees or woods, continues for a mile or two; messenger *appears* on bank, mildly rebuked and re-instructed: otter bobs up, have never seen another: fine enough river, most obliging *passage* thereon: we step out, thro' a notable decayed squire's mansion, now genteel farm; find gig in messenger's hands on the road; roll home; dine, and get packed and mounted again, over the moor to Youghal, the hospitable Currey still driving, still in all senses, carrying me along. Much talk with him: about the unquestionable confusion of leases; unreasons, good-efforts or otherwise of neighbour landlords; general state of men and things hereabouts; on all which he talks well, courteously, wisely. "Old Deerpark" (Duke's) on the height, bare enough of look; somnolent sunday hamlet, yet with people in sunday clothes some of them; somnolent bridge-keeper over muddy river, pleasantish road hitherto,—mount now to the moor-top, and ragged barrenness with many roofless huts is the main characteristic; wind rising to a proper pitch—Blackwater side very beautiful. Dromana &c seen over it. Squire's house hanging close with its lawnlet upon the edge of the high (seemed precipitous) river bank; fantastic-pretty in the sunny wind. Currey leaves letter there; meet Squiress and ladies walking in the grounds, Irish voices, pretty enough Irish ways of theirs. And so along, by deep woody dells, and high declivities, wild, variegated, sometimes beautiful, sometimes very ugly road, emerge at last upon the *final* reach of the Blackwater; a broad smooth now quite *tidal* expanse, and along the north shore of this by swift, level, often shady, course, to Youghal—" Yawal "—as they name it: a town memorable to my early heart—poor brother Alick's song of " *Yoogal* harbour" still dwelling with me, bringing whom now from *beyond* the ocean! Sun has about sunk: grey wind is cold. Youghal seen sheltered under its steep high ground; muddy, sooty, rather ugly look all has for such a fine natural scene. Long flat bare road at last, as if an embankment much of it. Halliday's stake nets, as used in Solway Firth; poor Halliday! "Captn Flash!" they sued him at law, put down *his* nets (he is now dead), sent him away and directly took to the *same* mode of fishing which still continues. Notable history of the " Bill for deepening Youghal Harbour " too; unreason, contradiction of neighbouring Sir This and Mr. That; patience of good quiet Duke—renewed unreason and misfortune. Y^l Harbour lies exactly of its old depth to this hour! Duke has here borrowed £10,000 of Government money to embank the marsh, and employ Y^l poor in famine year; which still goes on: good speed to it! Duke of Devonshire, and those he represents, I find eminent as " good landlords "—according to the commonly accepted *scale* of worth, they have been and are "good among the best." Bridge over Blackwater at Lismore; general style of management; here too, I found what was before visible, that the English Absentee generally far surpasses the native resident as an owner of land; and that all *admit* the fact indeed. What "a scale of worth" tho', must it be! Dingy scattered houses along a dingy waste, hungry, main-street full of idle sundayers; turn sharp to right up a lane close past a school founded by first Earl of Cork, past corner of "Sir Walter Raleigh's house" (now a quaker's), and in the cold dusty dusk we dismount in a little grassy court,—court of "Youghal College" (a kind of religious foundation, nobody could well tell me what); where, better or worse, an ancient pair of domestics received the tired travellers, light fire, get tea for them; and so taking leave of Currey, who is to start at 2 a.m. and do the impossible again to be at his grand jury work in Waterford, I mount to a big dim old room, the inner of two, and tumble into bed. Was there ever, for one thing, a more assiduous host than this Mr. Currey? He expected his wife to have met him here,— she is absent with her children, bathing-quarters some 7 miles off (Dungarvan bay perhaps?), but, owing to the mad state of the *posts* hereabouts just now, has never got his letter;—right hearty good night to him.

Monday 16th July.

After *two* sleeps, awoke to a bright day, in my welcome seclusion here at the back of Youghal dingy town. Strange place, considerable park, with old rugged trees, with high old walls, with rough grass and a kind of walk kept gravelly thro' and round it; leans up against the rapidly rising ground; roofs of the town and some quiet clean houses in the back street visible from the higher hillward part of the walk.—What can *be* the use of such a place? very mysterious; to me in my present humour very useful; most still forenoon passed wholly there. Servant, gruff but good, is an old English soldier, wife an old Youghal woman, who is much taken up with "Methodist Missions" in Ireland, for one thing; will have me to subscribe; I won't. Dim, half dilapidated, old house; my big room, big windows that shove up and give egress into the Park: still time, writing there; but about noon, (coach is to go about one or two); walk westward nearly the whole length of Ya'al; dingy semi-savage population; rough, fierce-faced, ragged, in the market place (or Quay) where the wares are of small mercantile value; ballad singer there. "Clock-gate" before that; and washed old humble citizen guides me into this square space of quay, or market, (if it were anything but some huckstering ragfair, with a few potatoes &c· in it); Post Office "no stamps;" home by the upper or northward range of lane, high on the hill edge, looking quite down upon the main street, to which again I descend. Wooden bridge, seen hastily yesternight, I hardly recollect at all. Coach, —fare 1 shilling "Opposition being hot"— some 33 miles; get away at last amid a rough miscellany, all or most of them however to *rear* of me. Gruff servant (his *son* I think brought my luggage) asks "are you for Derbyshire now, sir?"—thinking me bent straight for "the Duke." Crack, crack, through Clockgate (clock *standing,* as I had found); westward, sight of sea and ships on left; mount, inn; fairly up, out of dingy Youghal; Cable Island rises clear on the left, amid clear sea, in the windy summer sunshine; and we are fairly whirling on towards. Brisk black-eyed driver often whips behind, ridiculously often all the way.

Killeigh; poor village, brook at this end,

remember little of it; poor woman, who had got up beside me, takes to crying; her son, driving her *last* time she was here, is now buried in that churchyard. " God's will "—she gradually quieted herself; " bad times for poor &$^{c.}$" yes, but could or would tell me almost nothing about the details. Weltering wet black bogs *before* Killeigh; and sea getting distant, with crops, and scrags and bogs between us and it. Little memorable to Castle Martyr: broad trim little street of that, Ld Shannon's gate and park at west end. Ragged boys, brown as berries; tattered people everywhere in quantity, but I had now grown used to them. " Middleton "—I really thought they called it "*Mill*town"—remember its long broad street of good houses, its stream or two streams at west extremity, with big mills; distillery (I think) in the distance, now a subsidiary poorhouse, a frequent phenomenon in these parts. Country not quite bare, otherwise

I

scraggy, bushy, weedy, dusty, full enough of ragged people, not now memorable to me at all. Cork harbour, a long irregular Firth, *indenting* the land in all manner of irregularities for 10 or 12 miles, now begins to shew some of its lagoons and muddy creeks, *not* beautiful here; various castles &c. are on the left; on the left lies or lay Cloyne, (B^p Berkley's), but " we don't pass thro' it, sir." Evening is getting cloudy, coldish, windy; carts met, some air of real *trade*, alas! if you look, it is mostly or all meal sacks, Indian corn sacks,—poorhouse trade. I didn't in all Ireland meet one big piled carrier's cart, not to speak of carrier's waggon, such as we see here! " Barry's Court," somebody names for me on the left; square old pile (Raleigh, in Desmond's war of 1580); remember " Foaty " also, which looked rather like a sentry box in the wide flat, now opening *grey* in the windy evening, with the muddy meanders of Cork harbour labyrinthically indenting it. Cold, dusty, windy: steep height now on our left, clothed with luxuriant wood, nice citizen's boxes nestled there, miles of it (perhaps near 3); looks very well; and Cork itself, white-housed, through the twilight vapour, is now visible ahead. Long street of suburb; goodish houses; at last Cork itself. Lea bridge sharp to left; fine wide crowded street, like a small *Cork* " Portland Place," with fine shops &^{c}. to left again a little of this, " Wo-hp!" porter of Imperial Hotel is waiting—*has* heard of Duffy. I get letters, washing, mutton-chop for dinner, young Englishmen, —middies as I gradually discover, are rather loudly dining near me.—There gradually dining in the wholsomest way attainable, I read my letters (Duffy, out to dinner, not yet visible); and endeavour to enjoy, or failing that to endure. Walk on the streets with cigar; loud song of the Blind Beggar on Lea bridge; gave him a penny and stopt silently to listen, " Oah Kehristins may the Lard protec ye from the dangers av the night, and guide yer sowls &c. &c. and may ye never know what it is forever dark, and have no eyes—and for Kehroist's sake, lave a penny for the blind that can never see again !" All this, or something similar in expression, he *chaunted* in a loud deep voice, strange enough to hear for the first time in the streaming thoroughfare in the dusk. Rain slightly beginning now, I return; take to writing: near 11 o'clock,—announces himself " Father O'Shea !" (who I thought had been *dead ;*) to my astonishment enter a little greyhaired, intelligent-and-bred looking man, with much gesticulation, boundless loyal welcome, *red* with dinner and some wine, engages that we are to meet to-morrow, —and again with explosion of welcomes, goes his way. This Father O'Shea, some 15 years ago, had been, with Emerson of America, one of the *two* sons of Adam who encouraged poor bookseller Fraser, and didn't discourage him, to go *on* with " *Teufelsdröckh.*" I had often remembered him since; had not long before *re*-enquired his name, but understood somehow that he was dead;—and now! To bed, after brief good night to Duffy; and, for rattling of window (masses of pamphlets will not still it) cannot, till near 5 a.m., get to sleep at all.

Tuesday 17th July.

" Seven o'clock, sir!—Seven o'clock, sir!" this I wove for some time into my deep dreams; then had to awake to see a little bottle-brush headed " Boots " with thimble full of " warm water," who had marked me *wrong* " on his slate." Accursed " Boots"!—Dismiss him, almost like to assassinate him; but no sleep more; a miserable day for health, that; especially unfit to *walk* (ah me!) round by the Post Office (I suppose), by streets and quays after breakfast. Shallow stream (tide out) with high walls, somewhere off the main river, Statue of George II close by; market-place, rather squalid, miscellaneous; home and write till 2, when Duffy with " Denny Lane" enters. Happily I had *missed* all the forenoon's sights (schools, monasteries &c); am to go down the river by steam, and dine with Lane and a company, to sleep too— but that was altered at last—fine brown Irish figure, Denny; distiller—ex-repaler; frank, hearty, honest air; like Alfred Tennyson a little; goes and I write again till near four. Steamer then, and *our* company gathering amid the crowd on deck;—obliged to talk to this and the other: much rather *sit* and *look*. Beautiful white city, Cork, at the foot of its steep woody slope; at the head of its *indentive* narrow Frith, cutting its way thro' the hollows, making hills into *Islands,* for 10 miles up or more. Behind Cork, hilly country to sea, I suppose, but saw not—Sit on the paddle-box; stony-eyed friendly-professing Ulster Irishman (iron-monger, I think, but connected with Cork Newspaper) acting as "cicerone." Foaty &c" visible again; an open frith-indented plain. South westward (?) of the woody steep with its white country-houses; might be very beautiful, but is not yet. Down the Frith; passage, ill-whitewashed, weathered road; before that villas, some "Convent" the principal edifice. I saw out somewhere after passage; Lane waiting there, no time for Cove now; I drive back with stony-eyed-friend; get in some artificial walled establishment for that end, a saltwater bath. On then to Denny's cottage; which proves a small very crowded place, hanging over the sea-water, looking across towards Cove Island. Have to climb first (right *indisposed* for walking); kind Father O Shea going thro' his Hours, or doing something devotional, looking out like a living statue in a garden for some minutes after I came in sight; all priests' *duty* at certain hours: devotions done, statue Shea becomes live Shea, and cordially greets me again. Other priest, proprietor of garden, foolish rather, climbs with us, soon goes; and happily we are in Denny's and sit.

Dinner hospitable, somewhat hugger-mugger; much too crowded, old mother of D^y· Lane sat by me; next her, Father O'Something (*Sullivan* I discover in my letters). Shea's *Curate*, a Cork *wit*, as the punch soon shewed him; opposite me was Father Shea, didactic, loud spoken, courteous, good every way—a true gent^n & priest in the Irish style, my *only* good specimen of that. One Barry, editor of songs, of newspapers, next him; Duffy and two, nay 3 or 4 more, to left of me at the other end. O'Sullivan in yellow wig, man of fifty with *brick*-complexion, with inextinguishable good humour, caught at all straws to hang some light wit on them; really did produce much shallow laughter (poor soul) from me as from others; merry all; worth seeing for once, this scene of "Irish life." Out after sunset, take a boat, to Fort Carlisle, land at Cove; beautifulest still twilight: walk about Cove which seems much larger than I expected. Duffy recognized, "Mr Duffy there!" said some lad or girl, in the back or *upper* narrow Street. "Black thorn stick!" Phantasm in straw hat and rags, amid a small group of inhabit^s, all gone to black *shadows* at this hour, singing or acting some distraction, the burden of which was "Black thorn stick!" Some Irish modern Hercules, who helps himself divinely out of all difficulties by that. "Sure the craithurs are sick!" says he once, on some phenomenon or other turning up; then follows babblement quite unintelligible to me; but it is all cleared and cured soon as appears, by his "Black thorn stick!" Sootiest, most phantasmal piece of nonsense

I ever heard. To our boat again, Denny (ashamed of "Black thorn") dragging me off. Dark now; sea beautiful, and light still in it. Songs from two persons, editor Barry one of them; Father O'Sullivan, still witty, steering; (Father O'Shea had staid on land). "In hopes to harbour in thy arms!" was one of Barry's songs. "I-a-n ho-opes to ha-arbour in thy a-a-arms!" reiterates always some much enduring mortal of the sailing class;—and does get married, I think:—with a round of applause from us, and Cow joining in the burden. Round of applause done, Father O'S with a confidential business tone, mentions, "tho' joining faintly in the chorus, in the name of the Church I beg leave to protest!" this, with the tone, and yellow wig &$^{c \cdot}$ did well enough; a specimen of Father S^n. All priests almost, except Shea, surprise me by their seeming *carelessness* about religion, a matter of military drill with them, you would say. This cheery O'Sullivan, with his vulgar but real good humour was amongst the best I can remember, after the good O'Shea, who I hear labours diligently among a large poor flock; 3 or 4 curates : and though nothing of a bigot, seems truly a serious man. Home in 2 cars, O'Shea in mine ; jolty, dark, late, about 2 a.m. at Imperial Hotel (when a begging *idiot* starts up to *assist* us in ringing bell); we all part: sleep with difficulty 2 hours again ; not the *happiest* of men, no !

Wednesday 18th July.

Damp morning, yet with struggling sunshine; rejected contributor of Duffy's, sits at back table while we breakfast; speaks of L$^{d.}$ Limerick, of Dolly's Brae affair (quite new)—baddish fellow ; forgotten all but his *voice.* Three coaches in the road ; immense packing, get under way at last, towards Killarney and Shine Lawlor. Longish row of fellows *sitting* against the walls of houses on quay at the bridge end; very ugly in their lazzarone aspect under the sunshine. Spacious but half-waste aspect of streets as we roll upwards towards the hill country out of Cork. Windy, and ever more so; country bare. Put off *hat* (owing to head wind) at first stage, and took out *cap* from my carpet bag.—Bare commonplace country,—plenty of inequalities and "natural features," but culture, and elegance of taste in possessors, much wanting. Blarney Castle, I remember it, among its bit of wood at the foot of dingy uncultivated heights in dingy bare country; a grey square tower mainly, visible in its wood which the big waste seemed to reduce to a patch. Country getting barer, wilder; *forgotten* now, all details of it. Meet criminals, in long carts escorted by police; young women many of them, a kind of gypsey beauty in some of the witches, keen glancing black eyes with long coarse streams of black hair; "To Cork for trial"— eheu! Saw at another point of the road, large masses of people camped on the wayside, (*other* side of Mallow I think?) "waiting for out-door relief;" squalid, squalid, not the *extremity* of raggedness seen at Kildare, however. Remember next to nothing of the country; hedgeless, dim—moory, tilled patches in moory wilderness of untilled; heights in the distance, but no name to them discoverable, nor worth much search; wind freshening and right ahead. Mallow perhaps about two o'clock; hollow with modicum of woods; green all, and fertile-looking, with pleasant slate roofs and promise of a goodish town soon. Town really not bad: swift yet darkish stream as we enter; ascending street, shops, air of some business; barrack (fails nowhere): we *descend* again swiftly, street narrower and winding but still handsome enough; have to turn to Limerick Railway Station, and then amid the tumult of men, horses, boxes, cars, and multiplied confusion, wait long before we can return to hill-foot, and *resume* our road. Sheltered road for some miles; on our right over the hedge, runs ugly as chaos ditch of a *futile* "Canal." This is the way to Ballygiblin (Sir W. and Lady Beecher's), but I have given up that. Wind still higher, sunshine gone; haggard famine of beggars; (one stage I specially remember in this respect; poorest of hamlets, hungriest of human populations); dust, tempest, threatenings of rain; *cigars* are my one poor consolation: At "Millstreet" dine or lunch; pleasant village among woods on the hill-slope, as seen from the distance; interior, one mass of mendicancy, ruined by the "famine," by the potatoe-failure. All towns here seem to depend for their trade on mere produce of the earth: mills, distilleries, bacon, butter,—what of "respectability with gig" could be derived from that has taken station in towns, and all is wrecked now. After lunch, street filled with beggars; people in another coach threw halfpence; the population ran at them like rabid dogs, *dogs* of both sexes, and whelps; one oldish fellow I saw *beating* a boy, to keep at least him out of the competition. Rain; "Hay-y-p!" down hill at a rapid pace, happily we get away. Duffy has taken refuge inside; and the rain now for about an hour becomes furious;—lasts in furious occasional showers, but briefer, till near the end of the journey. Desolate, bare, moory country; hanging now in clear wet; much bog, mainly bog; treeless and swept over by a harsh moist wind; ugly, ugly, and very cold; meet drove of horses, coming from (or going to?) some "fair." Light clean-shanked cob-looking creatures, very cheap; I was told "£5" or so, for they are unbred and they are lean. Sharp-nosed pinched little Irishman with wild grey little eyes and dark hair has now (I really don't remember where) got upon the coach, is very explanatory, communicative;—a kind of caterer for some hôtel, as I gathered afterwards. That is "Mangerton" (a huge ugly hulk of a mountain truncated-pyramidal) with the Devil's Punchbowl on the top of it; *that* is the lake country; and Macgillicuddy's Reeks you see there (further westward, an irregular serrated ridge), the highest land in Ireland!" and so forth. A gentleman in dish-hat whom I had seen first in Mallow (Lawless, Lord Cloncurry's son as I learned afterwards) came now up beside me: civil English dialect, "had got *spoiled* potatoes to dinner yesterday at Mallow." Nothing memorable more. A fierce rain, where we changed horses, when he got up; wretched people cowering about to look at us, or beg, nevertheless: and this ended our rain for that evening. N.B. Lawless's former coach was somehow connected with the London undertaking (new this season) to forward or *frank* man to Killarney for a certain sum: one or two frankers I think he told me, were in that coach. Dim to me all of it,—and unimportant!

Mangerton, streak of Killarney evening smoke, and Macgillicuddy's serrated ridge, front of the mountain-country, handsomely fringed too with some wood, were now getting very visible; the moor changes itself into drained cultivated land, with gentlemen's seats, and human, or *more* human farmhouses: —decidedly rather beautiful, by contrast especially. Rain gone, wind tolerably fallen; western sky clear as *silver*, but mostly still overhung with dark waving sheets of cloud. "Inn, and a cup of hot tea;" that is the grand outlook! Big mills (I think?) at crossing of some stream; we are near some *castellated* modern house up on the left,—name forgotten, proprietor (useful, slightly squinting young man, connected with Peoble O' Keefe's territory) dined with us next day. High avenues, Lord Kenmare's; steepish descent; paved street at last, and square-built open street (town of 6,000 you would have said, 12,000 I was *told*); chaos of hungry porters, inn agents, lodging-agents,—beggars, storming round you, like ravenous dogs round carrion; this is Killarney. Swift, O swift into the car for " Roche's ", for anybody's; and let us off! Roche's, I find is a mile-and-a-half distant; at the lake side or near it; fine avenues all the way, and we go fast—the inn itself, a kind of general lodging house rather, did, in my experience, by no means correspond to our hope. Funeral overtaken by us; the " Irish howl;"—totally disappointing, there was no sorrow whatever in the tone of it. A pack of idle women, mounted on the hearse as many as could, and the rest walking; were hoh-hoh-ing with a grief quite evidently hired and not worth hiring. Swift, thro' it! Here is " Roche's," a long row of half-cottage looking buildings; in the middle part is the inn proper and we get admitted *taliter qualiter*. Bedrooms of the smallest ever seen " no private sitting room ;" bread bad, tea lukewarm,&c: public room (which happily is nearly empty) has no window that will come down in it, and to shove any up (or support it up) you must have a stick : evidently not the best ventilated or the best in any respect of terrestrial inns. I walked out, to be free of the hot foul air ; would fain have seen the lake or Mucruss Abbey at night without any guide,— but couldn't, no admittance anywhere. Rain beginning, I came in ; wrote a letter ; went to bed.

Thursday 19 July.

Bedroom reminds me of being tied up in a sack ; clean quiet little cell, however ; smoke out of the window, and look at the early sun and moon.—Moon turned away from Killarney. Shine Lawlor appears at breakfast: polite, quick, well-bred-looking, intelligent little fellow, with Irish-English air, with little bead-eyes and features, and *repale* feelings, Irish altogether. We are to come after breakfast, he will "shew us the lake," regrets to have no bed &c.—polite little man;—and we are to bring the *inn* car for ourselves and him. Poor S. L., perhaps he *had* no car of his own in these distressed times!. The evident poverty of many an Irish gentleman and the struggle of his hospitality with that, was one of the most touching sights;—inviting, and even commanding respectful *silence* from the guest surely; Shine Lawlor's "Castle-Lough" (I think he calls it) is a beautiful little place, in thick woods, close to "Roche's," and looking over the very lake,— though not from this parlour where we now were. *Shea* Lawlor there too, a kinsman from Bantry; tallow-complexioned, big, erect man, with sharp-croaking Irish voice, small cock-nose, stereotype glitter of smile, and small, hard blue eyes,—explodes in talking about Duffy; ex-repaler, talks *much*, half-wisely, whole-foolishly (I find) in that vein. "Rev^{d.} Dr. Moor, Principal of Oscot," high heavy man in black (catholic) gaiters; Catholic Harmonious Blacksmith,—really very like Whewell. Young Shine Lawlor's brother a *medicus* from Edinburgh; pleasant idle youth with cavendish tobacco: these are the party; Shine, Duffy, and I, off in car for "Gap of Dunloe," the others, all but Shea,—are to meet us in boat. Killarney workhouse; 3000 strong, the old *abominable* aspect of "human swinery"—managed as handsomely as they could. Rain has begun; Duffy turns, prefers to talk all day with Shea at Castle Lough: Shine and I alone; swift pleasant-enough colloquy; sensible, shifty man, has done his best in famine-time, with wretched tenants; still above water, thanks to "lying money" he had. Farm of his, "will you enter"? Yes. *Bare*, very bare, new cottage; built by farmer himself, who has a long lease; docks, puddles, with rubbish all round; kitchen place empty of furniture, except a stool or two, and some vestige of perhaps one table by the back-wall; sod roof visible from within; bearded, dirty, big farmer there, who stutters and is civil; worn little old wife; who is reluctant "to shew me her milk-house". How she keeps her milk? " I kape it in *keelers!* ";—with a haggard glance from the corner of her old black eyes. Daughter and she conduct us nevertheless; over wet cowhouse spaces from stepping stone to stepping stone; an ancient *cowhouse*, windows walled up with mortarless stones, no cows in *it*, milk in "keelers" (wooden *coolers*, shallow pails), standing two rows on the floor; sod-roof visible above has once had some smear of lime-wash, transient rat has rained down clay into some of the dishes; alas, alas! They supply the

Killarney workhouse with milk; have 40 cows (they say,—perhaps 40 *head:*) that is their farm industry. Fat stuttering farmer escorts us through spongy dock-field civilly to the road; and we mount again, and roll. " National School here, walk in ?" A most somnolent dusty establishment: perhaps some sixteen little scholars; unshaven sleepy schoolmaster, "*has* no best class," he says; —and indeed it is all a shrine of dusty sleep, among the worst of "National Schools;" not at all without rivals and even surpassers (victors in that bad race) as I found. "Outdoor relief" next; at a wretched little country shop; Shine's frank swift talk to the squalid crowd: dusty squalor, full of a noisy hum, expressing greed, suspicion, and *incarnated nonsense* of various kinds. Ragged wet hedges, weedy ditches; nasty ragged, spongy-looking flat country hereabouts;—like a *drunk* country fallen down to sleep amid the mud.

To left, up narrow hard moor-road here, hard like Craigenputtock country; beggars waiting at solitary corners, start with us, run sometimes miles,—get nothing, Lawlor doesn't mind them in the least. We are mounting fast into the stony hills; Macgillicuddy, not always very conspicuous, lies still further to the west (I think); this route is wholly westward of the lake. One beggar ran for 2 or perhaps 3 miles; he, on the dismissal of our car, does get coats &c. to carry, and a shilling I suppose. Ex-*repale* Shine does agree with me that a Parliament,—any Parliament in these times, is a mere talking-machine; that "Parliament in College-green," even if it could be had, is moonshine. Pass is getting straiter, high rocky brows on left hand; We dismiss our car, take to walking; mount now thro' the "Gap" itself; high rugged black cliffs, of slaty or *flag* structure lower overhead on both hands; with tumbled masses of the same below, and bright fat grass bordering them,—" grass which *kills* cattle" (when they get too *much* of it suddenly, I suppose!).—Melancholy small farm (with clean straw-roof however), where the gap *opens* into a kind of craggy wide-pit, and we are now at the summit of the place; wild grey damp sky, and showers still scudding about. In front of the farmhouse is " Dunloe hotel," so Shine laughingly names it. Squalid, dark, empty cottage, where with a dirty table and bench, without fire visible, food, or industry of any kind, sit two women to press upon you the " dainty of the country" " whisky and goat's-milk." Taste it; a greasy abomination; gave the wretches sixpence; and get away. Poor wretches, after all; but human *pity* dies away into stony misery and disgust in the excess of such scenes. One of these women is the farmer's sister; " he won't let me enter *his* house," she said or hinted; the other *mistress* of the vendible dainty, I learned afterwards, (at least if Irish carman's observation could teach) was "Kate Kearney's" niece; "Kearney" she too, but not of the song,—tho', if lifted from her squalor, she might be a handsome woman. Step along out of rocky circuit (amphitheatre would have *sloped* more); Shine talking of deer-hunts here; no other *stock* (heard of), unless it were that farmer's 2 or 3 small *kews* (cows). Other face of the wild, too, haggard misty glen (to right of us), and glens and hills; *boggy* looking; air of Galloway and Puttock. Path, for which we have left the road, is craggy; sharp showers fall; descend, descend; near the bottom we meet young Lawlor, find Catholic Harmonious Blacksmith waiting for us under the shelter of a little bridge: forward now to—boathouse (it proves), with gay boat, four dressed handsome native boatmen; and sherry &c.; lunch in it (as the oars go), of which I cannot eat, much preferring to smoke instead.

Lake clear, blue,—almost black; slaty precipitous islets rise frequent; rocky dark hills, somewhat fringed with native arbŭtus (very frequent all about Killarney), mount skyward on every hand. Well enough;—but don't bother me with *audibly* admiring it: Oh! if you but wouldn't! Come once or twice aground with our boat, in muddy creeks seeking the picturesque too eagerly; otherwise a pleasant sail. " Ornamental cottages," deep shrouded in arbŭtus wood, with clearest cascades, and a depth of *silence* very inviting, abound on the shores of these lakes; but *something* of dilapidation, beggary, human fatuity in one or other form, is painfully visible in nearly all. " Ornamental Cottage " first; woman had gone out to gain a halfpenny by opening a gate for us (but missed that somehow); within one window of the place, a grey fat *savant* is busy sticking dead beetles into his Natural History pocketbook with pins; rolls a big minatory eye on us as we pass; Kitchen next to him, where we enter, is squalling infant (mother out to gain halfpenny), rubbishy fireless floor with two other children;—ugly upon my honor! Stag-hunts have been; *yonder* (west side of the lake); most silent, solitary, with a wild beauty looking thro' the squalor of one's thoughts; that is the impression of the scene; moist, soft weather too harmonized. Boatman sings us, by order, two " repale songs;" deep bass voice, and business tone, songs obscurely *emblematic*, clearly of most ignorant character; a fine roman-nosed steel-complexioned fellow, the singer; who also awoke *echoes*, worth not much. I remember a most rapid *strait*, between black rocks, sometimes reckoned dangerous; item, an old black bridge (beggar-girls at it, " we been waiting for ye all day!"). Boatman steered—(song—boatman chiefly) and *shot* the lightened boat, we passing on foot, along the rapid rock-walled channel here. Dangerous this truly; especially in floods; gentleman (young Lawlor's acquaintance) drowned there, in spite of best swimming skill. We waited, in rain, below some other bridge (I remember till boat came up;) passed also below a wooden bridge (woody, wild, but pleasant country all this); and now we are in the *lower* lake, bigger but not so interesting. Land at some ornamental cottage called ———, where the people being understood to be at dinner we do not call; go on to "Lady Kenmare's cottage;" and return. Beautiful little cottage, "which her Ladyship never inhabits;" in the sweetest little woody bay or cove; mosaic pavement down to the water edge; grand *Swiss* projecting caves; bay windows &^{c}; All the floors and sofas *pealed,* if we look within; and for a finale a big stone has been hoisted through one of the glass-panes, which gapes there, wide as your hat, as if in sorrowful anger and surprise; "her Ladyship never visits it."

Alas, the futilities of man! Big lake is rather windy, even rough; some religious island with edifice (name forgotten) is visible in it to left or *north-west*. Mucross House (Herbert's) indistinctly, Mucross Abbey hardly at all, with woods and those bare Mangertons and mountains in front; pale brassy sky glitters cold on us, boat pitches, wind blows; one is hungry, and glad enough to reach Castle-Lough. Confused toilette; confused drawing room; dinner at last; squires, two doctors, two poor English ladies (M^rs. Lawlor and sister), quite "*subdued* to what they work in," not interesting, tho' really sad to me (what interest there was);— Harmonious (Catholic) Blacksmith was on one side (eupeptic, tolerably thirsty too), then Peoble O'Keefe (let us call him the *castellated* squire slightly squinting), Duffy and one or both doctors; I was on the other side, 2nd. English lady (knows "Bayswater" if nothing else) was mine, then Shea Lawlor, and perhaps another or two others. Dinner was noisy-Irish, not unpleasant, not anywhere unpolite ; nor was intelligence or candour (partly got up for me it might be, yet I think was not) amid the roughish but genial mirth a quite missing element. Shea talked largely, wanted *me* to open on O'Connell that he might hear him well denounced; but I wouldn't; Shine talked, workhouse labour &c, and Peoble O'Keefe talked ; bad tea in fireless parlour ; finally we emerge in pitch-dark night, with escort thro' the woods ; and bid our kind Irish entertainers a kind adieu. Good be with them, good struggling people ; that is my hearty feeling for them now.

Friday 20 July.

Good morning, with a pious "blessing" from our steel-complexioned boatman; who is waiting, as a crowd of others do, idle in front of "Roche's;" I have a *private* road, these two mornings, which leads unfrequented up to the hills—secluded smoke there, in the breezy sun. We are for Limerick road now; uncertain rather how. One Crosbie of Tralee has written inviting me, to whom I have written appointing notice from him *hither;* none has yet come. Public-car starts from Killarney at 11. Off we; meet postboy, no letter *yet*,—Crosbie of Tralee, is off then. Drive on to Shea Lawlor's in Killarney main-street, and consult about "King William's Town," and the possibilities of that. Quite possible;—start on car for that; will make "Castle-Island" after it to-night, and wait there for Limerick car or coach to-morrow. Jolt, jolt, (bad car); away, away!

Limestone quarry; steep ascent,—relief Com[n] road, to *improve* it, *walled up*, tho' nearly ended; one of many such we saw, in those parts chiefly. Scandalous wide moor begins, stretches ever wider, with huts and people ever more deplorable, for (I guess) some 15 dreary miles, "M⁣c⁣· Quag" or some such man's limework about the middle of that space; "hospitable man Mʳ· Mᶜ· Quag, sir." Has no *water pail*, however; some cranes, quarry heaps, and rude show of substance about him; other vestige of " productive industry" we saw nowhere. Road (" made by Queen Elizabeth ") runs straight as an arrow, over hill, over hollow; steep and rough, and unspeakably dreary; bare, *blue*, bog without limit, ragged people in small force working languidly at their scantlings or peats, no other work at all; look hungry in their rags; hopeless, air as of creatures sunk beyond hope, look into one of their huts under pretence of asking for a draught of water; dark, narrow, *two* women nursing, other young woman on foot as if for work; but it is narrow, dark, as if the people and their life were covered under a tub, or " tied in a sack "; all things smeared over too with a liquid *green;*—the cow (I find)

L

has her habitation here withal. No water; the poor young woman produces butter-milk; in real pity I give her a shilling. Duffy had done the like in the adjoining cottage, ditto, ditto in Charcuter, with the addition that a man lay in fever there. These were the wretchedest population I saw in Ireland. "Live, sir? The Lord knows; what we can beg, and rob," (rob means *scrape up;* I suppose?): Lord Kinmare's people, he never looks after them, "leases," worthless bog and I know not what. Bog all reclaimable, lime everywhere in it; swift exit to lord Kinmare and the leases, or whatever the accursed *incubus* is! The people, as I surmise, do *live* by "butter-milk;" wretched produce of a lean cow here and there, still alive upon the bog; pound or two of butter (precious stuff it must be in these huts!) Indian-meal, and there is sour milk over and above.

Good road at last, a broader one, and down swiftly by it to "King William's

Town," where are slated cottages, hedges, and little fields with crops and even cabbages in them; a blessed change indeed. Sad dilapidated inn,—potatoe-failure, and farther the poor landlady's broken heart (we find), " hardly in her mind since loss of her son." Here, at police barrack produce M$^{c\cdot}$ Gregor's circular; and all is made handy for us; and before we have dinner done, " M$^{r\cdot}$ Boyne," a jolly effectual-looking man of fifty, waits civilly upon us, has his car on the road, and will " shew us everything."

Peoble O'Keefe's country was confiscated in the rebellion of 1641; this huge tract of moor (part or whole of his territory) was, clandestinely at length let on many-lived leases to the O'Keefe representative (i. e. nominally to some other, in reality to him), of which the present specimen ("slightly squinting") had dined with us last night. Some 18 years ago, the many-lived lease ran out; rent had been some £45; question is, Let it again? Griffith of Irish Board of Works, backed by Lords Besborough and Monteagle (Spring Rice) then in office, got an answer, "No, try to improve it," and a grant, or successive grants, which have now run to £24,000 under the guidance of this Boyne, a Meath man, Land-surveyor's son, who had already "cut the Galtee mountains in four" by roads thro' them and was known by Griffith for an excellent "colonel of spademen" which he *is*. Boyne has now been 17 years there: a most solid, eupeptic, energetic, useful-looking man; whose *mark* stands indelible on this bog. "Couldn't stand without sinking here, when I first came"—excellent rye and oats growing now, hedges of thorn, bright copious green of grass, 100 head of "specimen cattle" (among others), clean cottage-farms; a country beautiful to eye and mind as we drove thro' it in the bright fresh evening. Boyne has a farm of (I think?) three hundred acres, or was it £150 a year; first-rate farm, first-rate dairy, &c., as we ourselves saw. His rent goes into the Government Grants; for he is yearly taking in new moor, only some 750 acres out of (5 or 6000?) being yet under plough and scythe. His cottagers, perhaps 30 or 40 with *farms*, had none of them quarrelled with him, tho' all had been *shifted* from their lots; they had brimless hats, even of dirty tanned skin, and had incidental tatters on their coarse clothing; but they looked healthy, hearty, swift and brisk, and even joyful, as we saw them at their labours,—decidedly the pleasantest aspect, or the only "pleasant" one, I can remember in Ireland. Brimless man, for example, issuing from the lime-kiln, dust wholly, but a pair of inextinguishably brisk healthy-eager eyes,—to solicit, with impetuous rapid eloquence, "some little of the ould turf to mix with the new," that it might burn better: granted! Other man near Boyne's potatoe-field; cottagers all, of still *better* expression. Boyne's own farm; his dairy the *best* (or equal practically to the best) I ever saw. Excellent "*rye*," "walk through it, gent^m., you wont hurt it!" as high as ones chin, thick, clean and regular, tho' the soil below seemed mere pieces of *peat*, which would have burnt still. Tea with Mrs. Boyne and him; excellent Dandie-Dinmont parlour, *personel* and entertainment altogether. But the expense, £24,000? B. admitted that it was immense; urged, however, what was true, that most of it had been laid out on *roads*, "being road to Kantuck," road to &^{c.} &^c, which was raising the value of *other* properties, of all properties; and that what he had laid out on this specially was *partly* returned to him,— almost *wholly*, as we computed from his *data;* though B. himself was candid enough to admit that if this moor were *his*, he would not take quite that method of reclaiming it, he would get good farmers and let it with improving leases."—" But if you had 2000 labourers already fed and clothed to your hand (such as sit in the Killarney workhouse idle at this moment)?"—Boyne's eyes sparkled; but his practical solid soul refused to admit so transcendent a speculation, and he did not dwell on that outlook. Moor enough nevertheless, worth little to any creature, *is* lying hereabouts for all the paupers in Cork county this half century to come; lord Kenmare or whatever lord or mortal obstructs that result, ought to be informed that he mus'nt!—positively! Anecdote of the late " Land Improvement Society." Bull about Limerick : " What price ? " asked B. " £20 "—" Pooh! will give you £8 "— Sec^y of Land Imp^t Society gave us £30 for the very fellow of it." "If you like to send it down from Limerick to King William's town within a week, I will give you £8 ;"—and it was *sent*. Land Improvement Society is now, naturally, *extinct* in bankruptcy. Remarkable Triptolemus, this Boyne.—Heavy broad man, fat big cheeks, grey beard well shaven; clean enough; smallish but honest kindly intelligent hazel-eyes and nice brows to his big round head, which he flings slightly back in speaking and rather droops his eyelids; Irish accent, copious *bubbling* speech in querulous-genial tone, wholly *narrative* in character. Simplicity, energy, eupepticity; a right healthy thick-sided Irish soul; would one knew of 1000 such. Catholic, I should think, but we didn't ask. Wife, a timidly-polite, yet sufficiently energetic-looking, rather beautiful woman of the due age; was recorded (by B. with oblique politeness) as admiring Duffy; had excellent *scones*, tea, cream and butter;—which ended, we, really with emotion and admiration, quitted Boyne-dom. Police-serj^t was there, who brought up our car for us; many thanks (*money*, said Duffy, will insult): and so off,—not now to Castle-Island and the Limerick coach or car; but to Kanturk (of like distance, and of more certain *inn*), by which from Mallow the Limerick *rail* would receive us. Kanturk, after long drive, restive horse, moors, cottages not very bad, some moor-burning &c.; Boyne's road getting ever dimmer, and at last quite dark. Newmarket, hill-village, after sunset, horse clear for stopping.—Spectral shadow as of a huge old gothic castle on our left, about a mile before Kanturk: somebody's "Folly," the carman assured us, and a modern thing; long slumbering street of suburb; broader street, then, solitary watchman bawling with the old asinine-leonine voice "ha-alf past wan-n-y!"? and high at the head of the street rises with immense flight of steps our high "hotel," where, in a dim, drowsy, not too comfortable manner, we hustle ourselves into beds and sleep. Duffy (loyal soul, as always) yielded me by far the best room;

but even it, except for size, could by no means be called good.

Saturday 21 July.

Good enough morning; sun gradually getting out; walk thro' Kanturk, to find somebody who can give some reliable information about Mallow rail trains; difficult, but find one at last, a grocer or spirit dealer, and return. Kanturk shaped like a Y; our hotel at the bottom of the broad stalk of the " Y ;" rivers, shallow, broad, pebbly but none of the cleanest, intersect the other two branches; " their names ? " man in street can't tell me. —See guide-book if one likes! I have decided now to *go* by Lady Beecher's and Ballygiblin; Duffy, in route to Mallow, can set me down at their gate; and we are to rendezvous in Limerick, at the chief hotel. Newspaper vendors, curious-impertinents;—after various delays we do depart. Pleasant country, hill and hollow and no longer moory; culture tolerable in general. Horse's saddle needs *repair;* beggar-woman; clean cap, sincere-looking creature.—Duffy's shilling. " Lady Beecher's schoolhouse," then Ballygiblin gate; soon after noon I think; and there I am left, walking pensive, in a grey genial day, thro' a fine park, half a mile, towards this unknown mansion. Two letters I had, one from A'ʸ· Sterling to Lady, one from Lord Monteagle to Sir W., and these, for I think I was hardly known otherwise, except by alarming rumour (heterodoxy &ᶜ·) procured me handsome admittance.

Lady B.⁶ a tall stately leanish figure of 55; of strict, hard aspect, high-cheek bones, and small blue eyes,—expression of vigour, energy, honesty; tone of voice, and of talk, dry, stinted-practical. Luncheon with two of her youths just setting off for Killarney, a dᵒ that

⁶ Lady Beecher had been Miss O'Neill, the famous actress.

was to stay, and her two young ladies—handsome fair skinned fine-featured people all; quite English in type and ways. House and grounds beautiful; school, cottages, peasants, all in perfect order;—walk with Lady B.—and then with Sir W's brother (" Wrixon " is the original name, " Beecher " was adopted for *heritable* reasons). All things trim and nice, without doors and within; as in the best English or Scotch houses of the kind. A strict religionist, Lady B., really wholesome and worthy, easy enough to talk with, nor quite unproductive; her *boudoir* by the side of the hall, father and mother's portraits in it; and all manner of lady-elegancies; people meeting her " mylady-ing, the boy is better-ing;" everything has been subdued to herself, I find, and carries the image of her own strict methodic vigorous character, and perfect Church of Englandism, which I find she zealously adopts as the exponent of this universe, and struggles continually to make serve her as a complete rule of life. Very well indeed.—Sir W. much lamed now (by some fall from his horse) appears towards dinner; fine mildly dignified old gentleman, reminds me of Johnstone of Grange. Evening pleasant enough; one young lady plays me innumerable Jacobite tunes; rest of the party playing whist; Lady B. herself ended by singing me "Bonny Prince Charlie." To sleep, in excellent room and bed; a place where one *can* sleep,—infinitely grateful to me.

Sunday 22 July.

Dim breezy morning. Train doesn't run to Limerick to-day; must stay, am as well pleased!—Decide to give Duffy leave to go himself,—and do so in the afternoon; one of various notes I wrote there. To Church in the meanwhile; walk with Mr. Wrixon, Sir

W B's brother, a farmer on his own account, and general manager, as I can gather, at Ballygiblin; Lady and Sir are in the big old carriage by some circuitous road. Sudden change, in passing a hedge as we walk along the highway: what is this? Lord Limerick's estate; ground untilled some of it, thistles, docks, dilapidated cottages, ragged men; two years troublous insolvency, and now they are *evicted:* " here is one of them; I will just set him going for you; turn the spigot, and he will run all day!" Middle-aged farmer-peasant, accordingly, takes off his hat, salutes low, walks hat in hand, wind blowing his long thick hair, black with a streak of grey. His woes, his bad usages. I distinguish little but at all turns " tham vagobonds!" he has been fellow sub-lessee of lands along with various other " vagabonds;" he paid always to the nail, they not; all are now turned out into the road together, the innocent along with the guilty; kind neighbour has taken *him* in, with wife and children, for the time. A reasonably good kind of man, to appearance, and in the truest perplexity, with laws of the truest injustice. "And have you any notion what you are to do now?" "Not a ha'p'orth, yer honour!" Mr. W. can give no work, wishes he could; the poor man will write to Mr. Somebody (the agent) at Cork, begging passage to America, begging something or other. W. will ratify his respectability;— and so we make away, and leave him to clap on his hat again. Sad contrast continues; ugly cottages, unploughed lands, all gone to savagery;—poor-house alone like to reap much produce from this kind of culture. Lord Limerick's method, and his father's before him. Loud and very just complaint that a Beecher should be tied to a Limerick in this way; not left to swim the gulph of pauperism separately, but obliged to do it together! A universal complaint; quite tragic to see the justice of, everywhere;—Larcom and his men are doing what they can to help it; which practically is but little hitherto.

Church service; clean congregation of 40; redhaired young Irish parson, who is very evidently " performing " the service. Decency everywhere; poor little decent Church with the tombs round it, and a tree or two shading it, (on the top of a high rough-green bank with a brook at the bottom): service here, according to the natural English method, " decently performed." I felt how decent English Protestants, or the sons of such, might with zealous affection like to assemble here once a week, and remind themselves of English purities and decencies and gospel ordinances, in the midst of a black howling Babel of superstitious savagery—like Hebrews sitting by the streams of Babel:— but I feel more clearly than ever how *impossible* it was that an extraneous son of Adam, first seized by the terrible conviction that he had a soul to be saved or damned, that he must rede the riddle of this universe or go to perdition everlasting, could for a moment think of taking this respectable "performance" as the solution of the mystery for him! Oh, Heaven, never in this world! Weep ye by the stream of Babel, decent clean English-Irish; weep for there is cause, till you can do something *better* than weep; but expect no Babylonian or any other mortal to concern himself with that affair of yours! And on the whole I would recommend you rather to give up "weeping,"— take to working out your meaning rather than weeping it. No sadder truth presses itself upon one than the necessity there will soon be, and the call there everywhere already is, to *quit* these old rubrics and give up these empty performances altogether. All "religions" that I fell in with in Ireland seemed to me too irreligious; really, in sad truth, doing mischief to the people in place of good! —Our ladies joined zealously in the responses, the gentlemen too kept up a form of following, but were passive rather. Home in the carriage, good "moral talk" with Lady B. whose hard eyes have a good deal softened towards me. Note-writing,—then I think an hour of sleep (the afternoon proved showery, with high breezes); at half past six to dinner: young red parson (decent vacuity); *other* brother of Sir W's, *unhealthy* parson who has revenues and keeps a curate,—talk of wonderful Scotchman, who " *built* Fermoy;" that is, first made it something of a town. Anderson (I think? perhaps not?); a Scotch pedlar boy, expanded himself by slow steady degrees; took to trading on the great scale, to running coaches; set up a bank; became Bar^t. but *failed* (not dishonourably); son still lives, an *idle* undistinguished Bar^t., he. What the latter part of our evening was I hardly recollect at all: autobiography came on the carpet; I spoke with Lady B. now quite softened to me, and her fears hushed, about writing down *her* life; dry feeble laugh of gratification in reply, and talk enough, (tho' in quite general terms) about her life as an actress. The big picture of Juliet (of which I remembered engravings from my boyhood) hung conspicuous in the drawing-room. Bed at last, not very late;—red parson and all have vanished in a grey sea of oblivion and sleep.

Monday 23 July.

Some difficulty about a car for me to railway at 2. Sir W. and brother at length take me in their carriage; 8 miles, not unattended with rain-showers. Commonplace green country, with weedy fields, ragged hedges, many brooks and boggy places; here and there a big mill,—the only kind of efficient manufactory one sees in Ireland, that of corn into meal. The meal too is *bad*, not well made generally but quite ill: the mill however is *large* enough;—there is surely a potentiality of good meal! To the station just in time; amid fierce scuds of wet, kind and polite farewell; and the steamhorse snorts away for Limerick; "Hah! Sir W$^{m.}$?" cried a lean old spectre of a gentleman in the carriage by me; but we were off, and there could be no interview—probably better so, I thought. Spectral old gentleman all gone but the *eyes*, set in a pair of baggy parchment cheeks, was willing to have talked, but I wouldn't: a Cork quasi-naval old spectral gentleman, full of windy hungry folly, after grouse just now. Silence much preferable! Foolish gabble about Queen's coming, and other as important topics. Green commonplace country; remember little of it, even of the latter part which they call "Golden Vale" so brazen did it look, in that sad humour. Remember the sound "Buttevant Station!" and sight perhaps of a barrack and some roofs on the right; item "Charleville," roofs, chapel &$^{c.}$ rather grey-looking;

on the left, "Kilmallock?" Yes, a black old haggard ruin, some monastery or other, amid black hungry-looking houses, visible for some time on the left; Galtee mountains on the right,—actual "Galtees" here, big block of peaky mountain country, Kilmallock, and onward, a Desmond country; *à la bonne heure.* Junction of Dublin-and-Limerick Railway; *we* are on the Cork-and-Limerick: long jumbling to and fro', on open platform; *put out* my cigar (in uncertainty for time), might have finished it well enough. Acquaintances of parchment spectre; "Irish "squireens," not of the best physiognomy. Off at last,—Catholic Harmonious Blacksmith, I see, is in the train, 2$^{nd.}$ class; quite affectionate he, but shy speaking much with him. Confused "Stations;" country green with some wood; hills northward, "Slieve Phelim" I fancy: white chateau among woods; spectral gentleman will know whose it is,—*was* somebody's, *is* a workhouse now, sir " Hah, Ah ! " Symptoms of Limerick at last, in the blessed showery afternoon.

Long low street, parallel to our rail; exotic in aspect, $Lim^{k.}$ plebs live there.— Station, strait confused; amid rain;—and poor Duffy stands there, with sad loving smile, a glad sight to me after all; and so in omnibus, with spectre, blacksmith, and full fare of others,—(omnibus that *couldn't* have a window opened) to "Cruise's Hotel,"— Cruise himself, a lean eager-looking little man of forty, most reverent of Duffy, as is common here, riding with us. Private room ; and ambitious—bad dinner, kickshaws (sweet breads, salmon &^{c}) and uneatables. Rich$^{d.}$ Bourke has at once followed me into my bedroom, an old London acquaintance busy here in Poor-law ; am to join him at Lisnagry to-morrow for dinner.—Strelezki and Inspector ; from them and Bourke, I have rapidly had to get loose for dinner.

Wet chief street of Limerick, glimpse of harbour, with poor turf-craft, mainly thro' an opening on the other side. Sickly, weary; Duffy reads *choice* Irish ballads to me,— unmusical enough. Priest O'Brien, he that roused the mob against Mitchel last year, a brandy-faced, pock-marked, very ugly man, of Irish physiognomy, comes in, with wild-eyed, still more Irish younger priest, and some third party of the editorial sort whom I do not recollect at all—Tea with these; and copious not pleasant talk. A baddish kind of priest; get out at last to find Strelezki (brush-headed, bell-voiced, busy little Pole whom I have seen in London) and the fat Inspector with whom he is dining. Further end of main street—which is very solitary and dim-looking now about 10. Find it at last; Pole gone; Inspector there, most civil, but little good to be got of him except *addresses* of the De Veres. Home and met O'Brien, Brandy face & C$^{o.}$ on the stairs:

Good night. O yes good night, and power to your elbows all! Slept considerably, not sufficiently.

Tuesday 24 July.

Towards post-office; *damp*-sunny morning: letters had come last night; other to day from "Inspector of Kilrush"; come, oh, come! Glove shop; Limerick gloves, scarcely *any* made now; buy a pair of cloth gloves; n. b. have my gutta-percha shoes out *soleing* with leather, gutta having gone like toasted-cheese on the paving in the late hot weather; right glad to have leather-shoes again! Breakfast bad; confused inanity of morning, settling, &c, about noon Duffy goes away for Galway; and I am to follow after a day. Foolish young Limerick philosopher,—a kind of "Young Limerick" (*neither* Old nor Young Ireland), in smoking room (wretched place), smokes with me while Duffy is packing to go; shewed me afterwards the locality of the Mitchel-and-Meagher tragi-comedy, and ciceroned me thro' the streets.

Engineer de Vere not in his office when I called in the morning; does not get return call. Quaker Unthank at $3\frac{1}{2}$ p. m.; lean triangular visage (kind of "Chemist," I think), Irish accent, altogether English in thought, speech and ways. Rational exact man; long before any other I could see in those parts.—At four, according to appointment, Bourke's gig with a lad; I decide to leave De Veredom then, to itself; and from Lisnagry *not* look back. Have walked about Limerick what I could; broad, level, strong new bridge, *better* kind of ships lying below it; Government Grants, and works, hear enough about these in reference to this Shannon concern! River broad, deep I suppose, drab-colored, by no means over-beautiful. Back street, on hill top, parallel to main one; here all the *natives* seem to congregate. Ragged turf-burning, turf-dealing long narrow street.—*Irish name* of it forgotten. Other narrow turf-dealing, potatoe- and-cabbage dealing poor streets, a crowded dingy population here; at length turn downwards again to left,—narrowest of *lanes* (was that *here?*) and drunk man with two poor women leading him;—finally down to the river-side again; I think, near a kind of *Island* in it. Big dark brown hulk of an edifice; what they call Cathedral,—bless the mark! Police barrack, round fantastic kind of building, which was once something far grander,—some projector's folly (ruined savings bank?) which I have now forgotten. —Adieu to Limerick by a broad open road, with some miserable little peat carts on it and nearly nothing else at all. Hardy intelligent lad; farmer's son on Sir Rich$^{d.}$ (Bourke's father's) ground; brother a schoolmaster; family *didn't* famish in famine-time having some resources;—he himself is engaged with

Sir R'ˢ· "Scotchman" Mʳ· Meall (from John *Mill's* country, I afterwards found), "to learn farming," 3 years at 2/6 a week. Very well.—Sir Lucius O'Brien's place; green, with *wood* shading the road near it. Lisnagry, "Blind farmer" (only docks and nettles, pay no rents); one Browne's, who *will* turn them away now: "no fear of being shot"— *was* shot at; got policeman, humour fallen now and less fear. Very ugly this particular spot. How a man "prints his image" here on the face of the earth; and you have beauty alternating with sordid disordered ugliness, abrupt as squares in a chess-board! So, all over Ireland. Sir Richard, nor any Bourke, not here; polite young Englishman visitor, in dish hat, steps out to do the honours; at length young Bourke himself, Old Bourke, two ladies (Mʳˢ· and Miss,—Scotch one of them, immemorable both); and the evening, in small polite parlour and dining room, passes tolerably enough. Card from

Engineer de Vere. Yes; no matter now. Settle to abide *here* over the morrow, and if I *can*, sleep, or at least lie horizontal all day; next day with Bourke to Gort, and thence Galway.

Wednesday 25 July.

Sir Rich$^{d.}$ Bourke, a fine old soldier, once Gov$^{r.}$ of New South Wales, man of 75 or 80; rises at 6, but is not visible, has his own hours &$^{c.}$. Something still military, mildly arbitrary, in his whole household-government (I find), and ways of procedure. Interesting kind of old Irish-British figure. Lean, clean face hacked with sabre scars and bullet scars; inextinguishably lively, grey bead-eyes, head snow-white; low-voiced, steady, methodic and practical intelligence, looks thro' his existence here. Bought this place on his return, 30 years ago; a black bare bog then; beautifully improved now, shaded with good wood, neat little house and offices, neat walks, sunk-fences, drains and flourishing fields; again the "stamp of a man's image." Dispensary, chapel, near the gate,—already bare and unbeautiful there; the "image" of the country and people, there, not Sir R^s· image. I smoke, and lounge about the grounds, all morning, having breakfasted with "Master Richard" who is off to Limerick for the day. Welcome enough solitude. The two ladies kind and polite, d^o· the young Englishman :—solitude is preferable.

In the afternoon, Sir R^d·, I beside him on the box, drives us. Lord Clare's place, the chief object;—large park, haymaking; big block of a house; gardens very greatly taken care of,—women washing the greenhouse, (Lordship just *expected*); quincunxes, foreign bushes, whirligigs; thought of his Lordship what he *was*, and felt all this to be a kind of painful *mockery* for a soul so circumstanced. First Earl Clare (father) a Fitzgibbon, lawyer,

Chancellor did the "Union;" a sorry jobber (I supposed); son of a d°·, some squireen of trading talent; and now it has come to this, as the finale!—Old soldier as gatekeeper, Sir R. and he salute, as old friends. To O'Brien's bridge (by the low road,—woody with occasional glimpses of the river); Village, white; lower end of it pretty, in the sunshine; upper part of it squalid, *deserted* mostly: relief-work road,—*half* breadth cut away, and so left: duckwood ditches, drowned bog, inexpressibly ugly for most part, some cleared improved spot, abruptly alternating with the drowned squalor which produces only bad brown stacks of peat. Sir R$^{d.}$ in mild good-humour trots gently along. Two drunk blockheads, stagger into a cross road to be alone; are seen *kissing* one another as we pass,—just Heaven, what a kiss, with the drowned bog, and gaping full ditches on each hand! Long meagre village, hungry single street "Castle Connell"—?

Sir Richard's man has been at a fair with sheep (" Six-mile-bridge ?"), is met or overtaken here: "prices so and so, rather bad." —Home; wait for " master;" dinner and evening have much sunk with me into the vague, and are not much worth recalling. Talk from Sir Richard about wonderful viaducts, canals, and industrial joint-stock movements, seen and admired by himself, done during Louis Philippe's time. Good for something, then, that royal Ikey-Solomons? Most things are good for *something:*—out of a slain hero you will at least, if you manage his remains at all, get a few cartloads more of turnip-fodder; ach Gott! Bed, I forgot how; I had slept during forenoon for a little, and now slept better or worse again.

Thursday 26 July.

Spent the morning, which was damp yet

with sunshine, in lounging about the shrubberies and wooded alleys; expected Bourke would have been ready to set out before noon, instead of not till 2 p.m. or thereabouts, as it proved. Group of ragged solicitants, this morning and the last, hung about the front-door, in silence for many hours, waiting "a word with his Honour"; tattery women, young and old; one ragged able man; his honor safe within doors, they silent sitting or standing without, waiting his Honor's time, tacit bargain that no servant was to take notice of them, they not of him; that was the appearance of it. Sad enough to look upon; for the answer, at last, was sure to be "can't; have no work, no &c. for you: sorry, but have *none!*" Similar expectants in small numbers I had seen about Sir W. Beecher's: probably they wait about most gentlemen's houses in Ireland in this sad time. Glanced over newspapers; at length out with young Bourke (who is taking the " management," I find, his father surrendering as " too old ") ; went with him to the scene of Scotchman Meall's operations ; scouring a big ditch, several men up to the knees throwing out duckweed, and bog mud,—once a year. Wood around, and good crops, provided you *keep* the ditch scoured ; all this region, by nature, execrable, drowned bog : let the cutting of turf by measure ; turf once all cut away, attack the bottom with subsoil and other ploughs,— water carried off, prospers admirably. Meall a good solid Angus man ; heavy Scotch qualities ; getting excellent farm-house and offices set up. Infested by *rabbits*, which eat young green-crop, young hedges (?) ; must have ferrets or weasels, and how?, Meall's labourers " do very well *if* there is one set to look at them ;" Hasn't yet got them trained to work faithfully alone, tho' making progress in that direction. Home in haste from Meall's farm and nice new gooseberry garden;—off actually at last, Limerick car long waiting.

Up the river; hills of Clare, hills in Limerick county; wide expanse, not without some savage beauty, far too *bare*, and too little of it absolutely green. Talk of Browne and his " blind farmers." Assassination of a poor old soldier he had sent to watch a certain farm; ominous menace before hand, then deed done, " done with an axe," no culprit discoverable. Killaloe, Bourke's house across the river among rather ragged woods. " City " (I think with some high old church towers) standing high at the other end of the bridge, in dry trim country, at the foot of the long lough, was pleasant enough from the *outside*,— one small skirt of it was all we travelled over. Lough now, with complex wooden and other apparatus for dispersing water; part of the questionable " Navigation of the Shannon." Questionable; indeed everywhere in Ireland one finds that the " Government," far from stinginess in public money towards Ireland, has erred rather on the other side; making, in all seasons, extensive *hives* for which the *bees* are not yet found. West side of Lough Derg: pleasant smooth-dry winding road. Clare hills stretching up, black-fretted, and with spots of culture, all treeless to perhaps 1500 or 2000 feet, gradually enough, on the left. Greener high hills on the other side of lake with extensive slate quarries, *chief* trade hereabouts. One *Spaight* of Limerick, able active man heard of before, works them; resides here. "St. Patrick's purgatory!" said Bourke, pointing out a flat island, with black tower and architectural ruins:—not *so*, (as I found afterwards: the Lough Derg of purgatory (still a place of pilgrimage, where Duffy with his mother had *been*) is in Donegal; smallish lough, some miles to right as we went from Sligo to town of Donegal. Hail shower, two policemen, on the terrace of the stony hills.

A country that *might* all be very beautiful, but is not so, is bare, gnarled, craggy, and speaks to you of sloth and insolvency. "When every place was no place, and Dublin was a shaking bog;" Irish phrase for the beginning of time. "Sitting under de ditch, taking a *blast* of de pipe;" Scotch this too, all but *ditch*, which doesn't as here mean *wall*-fence but *trench* for fence or drain.

Scariff; straggling muddy avenues of wood begin to appear; woman in workhouse yard, fever-patient we suppose; had come flat, seemingly without pillow, on the bottom of a stone-cart; was lying now under blue cloaks and tatters, her long black hair streaming out beyond her—motionless, outcast, till they found some place for her in this hospital. Grimmest of sights, with the long tattery cloud of black hair.—Procession next of workhouse young girls; healthy, clean in whole coarse clothes; the *only* well-guided group of children visible to us in these parts,

—which indeed is a general fact. Scariff itself, dim, extinct-looking hungry village (I should guess 1,000 inhabitants) on the top and steep sides of a rocky height. Houses seemed deserted, nothing doing, considerable idle groups on the upper part (hill top) of the street, which after its maximum of elevation spreads out into an irregular wide triangular space,—*two* main roads going out from it, I suppose, towards Gort and towards Portumna.—Little *ferrety* shopkeeper, in whole clothes, seemingly chief man of the place, knows Bourke by often passing this way; " Well, M$^{r.}$ (O'Flanahan, say, tho' that was not it), do you think we can get a car to Gort ? "—" Not a car here, sir, to be had for love or money ; people all gone to adjourned assizes at Tulla, nayther horse nor car left in the place ! " Here was a precious outlook : Bourke however did not seem to lay it much to heart. " Well M$^{r.}$ O'Flanahan, then you must try to do something for us ! ". " I will,"! cried the little stumpy ferret of a man; and instantly despatched one from the group, to go somewhither and work miracles on our behalf. Miracle-worker returns with notice that a horse and car can (by miracle) be achieved, but horse will require some rest first. Well, well; we go to walk; *see* a car standing; our own old driver comes to tell us that *he* has discovered an excellent horse and car *waiting* for hire just next door to M^{r.} O'Flanahan's. And so it proved; and so, in five minutes, was the new arrangement made; O'Flanahan acquiescing without any blush or other appearance of emotion. Merely a human ferret, clutching at game, hadn't caught it. Purchased a thimbleful of bad whisky to mix in water in a very smoky room from him; "odd copper, yours." "Why sir?" and sent ardently for "change," —got none, however, nor spoke more of getting. Poor O'Flan, he had got his house new floored; was prospering, I suppose, by workhouse grocery-and-meal trade, by secret pawnbroking,—by *eating* the slain. Our new car whisked us out of Skariff, where the only human souls I notice at any industry whatever, were two, in a hungry-looking silent back-corner languidly engaged in sawing a butt of extremely hard Scotch fir.

Road hilly but smooth, country bare but not boggy; deepish narrow stream indenting meadows to our left just after starting,— (mountain stream has made ruinous inundation since),—solitary cottages, in dry nooks of the hills: girl *dripping* at the door of one a potful of boiled reeking greens, has picked one out as we pass, and is zealously eating it; bad food, great appetite, extremity of hunger, likely, not unknown here! Brisk evening becomes cloudier; top of the country,—wide waste of dim hill country, far and wide, to the left: " Mountains of Clare." Bog round us now; pools and crags: Lord Gort's Park wall, furze, pool, and peatpot desolation just outside; strong contrast within. Drive long, after a turn, close by this park: poor Lord has now a "receiver" on him; lies out of human vision now! Approach to Gort: Lord Something-else (extinct now, after begetting many bastards), it was he that planted these ragged avenues of wood,—not quite so ugly still as nothing; —troublous huggermugger aspect, of stony fields and frequent, nearly all, bad houses, on both sides of the way. Haggard eyes at any rate. Barrack big gloomy dirty; enter Gort at last. Wide street sloping swiftly; the Lord Something-else's house — quaintish architecture, is now some poorhouse, subsidiary or principal; Bourke, on the outlook, sees lady friend or cousin at window, looking for him too, and eager salutations pass. Deposits me in dim big greasy-looking hôtel at the bottom of the street; and goes,—I am to join him (positively!) at tea.

Dim enough tea, lady is poor-law inspector's

sister wife or something. Poor-law Inspector himself is Bishop Horsley's son (or else grandson?); Dundee man, well enough and very hospitable, not a man to set the Thames on fire. Horrible account of chief inn at Galway; no good water attainable in Galway, no nothing almost! " Military ball *has* lately been at Gort; Gort too, in spite of pauperism's self, is alive;—" surgeon of the Regiment a Dumfries man?" well and good, *ach Gott!* Home to bed; snoring monster in some other room; little sleep; glad that it was not wholly none. [Be quick!]

Friday 27 July.

Up early enough, breakfast d°; wait for Limerick-&-Galway Coach, due about 8 a.m. (or 9?)—Confused ragged aspect of the market-place, on which (a second long street here, falling into the main one from westward, but *not* crossing it) my windows look, my bedroom window *has* looked. Sour milk firkins, sordid garbage of vegetables; old blue cloaks on women, greasy-looking rags on most of the men, defacing the summer sun, this fine morning! Troop of cavalry in undress file in from an easterly entrance,— exercising their horses; very trim and regular they. Good woman in silent tobacco-shop; what strange unvisited islands do, not uninhabited, lie in the big ocean of things! Chapel; people praying in it, poor wretches! Coach at last: amid tumult of porters, suddenly calling me, luggage *already* hoisted in, this man to pay and then that; Horsley too out saluting me, I do get aloft, and roll gladly away.

Some green fields, even parks and trees, tho' rather roughish, and with barren hills beyond, this lasts for a mile or two: then fifteen miles of the stoniest barest barrenness

I have ever yet seen. Pretty youth mounts beside, polite enough in his air and ways, not without some wild sense; "Connaught young gentleman", he too is something: on the box sits a fat Irish tourist in oilskin, beyond my own age; eager to talk, has squireen tendencies; no sense or too little; don't. "Connaught rangers 88th·, memorable to me for repute of blackguardism in Dumfries: natives proud of them for prowess here. Big simple driver, d° d° guard: I think we had no further company, and in the inside there was none. Stone cottages, stone hamlets, not nearly so ugly as you might have looked for in such a country,—stony, bare, and desolate beyond expression. Almost interesting as the breezy sunshine lay on it: wide stony expanse, in some places almost like a continuous flagged floor of grey—white stone; pick the stone up, build it into innumerable little fences, or otherwise shove it aside, the soil, when free, or freed of water, seems sharp and good. Parks here and there; where wood has thriven: greenest islets in the sea of stone. Martin of Galway's representative, in one; Browne or Black (Blake); plenteous names these. English-Irish air in all *our* company, Redington's (secretary) draining, trenching goes on here; our stage, and I see that my writing case *is* inside, beneath a big corn-bag. Galway bay, and promontory, where Galway city is. Stones, stones,—with greenest islets here and there. Oh for men, pickmen, spademen, and masters to guide them! "Oranmore," with grey masses of old monastic architecture. (Clanricarde's *Castle* this!). Silent as a tomb otherwise: not a hammer stirring in it, or a bootfall heard, stagnant at the head of its sleeping tide-water: how on earth do the people live? Barest of roads towards Galway: dusty, lonely, flanked by ill-built dry stone walls, poor bare fields beyond. Pauper figures, and only a few, the women all with some red petticoat or something very red, plodding languidly here and there under the bright noon; tatterdemalion phantasm, "piece of *real* Connaught," with some ragged walletkins on him, at a turn under some trees. Park*lets*, as if of Galway merchants; very green indeed, and wood growing bravely when once tried. Galway suburbs; long row of huts mostly or all thatched,—true Irish houses, "Erasmus Smith's school"; young gentleman knows of it; to the right; a big gaping house;—in vacation just now. Road always mounting, has now mounted, got into *streets;* gets into a kind of central square;—Duffy visible; Hotel (all full of assize people); and here are letters for me, a Galway editor for guide,[7] with car ready for yoking,—and we must be in Tuam *this* evening.

Letters read, we mount our car: straight steep streets, remarkable old city; how in

[7] His name Edward Butler, afterwards Attorney-General in New South Wales.

such a stony country it exists! Port wine and Spanish and French articles inwards, cattle outwards, and scantlings of corn; no *other* port for so many miles of country; *enough* of stony country, even that will make a kind of feast. Inlet of river from Lough Corrib the Connemara country: extensive government works here too. "Godless College," turreted grey edifice, just becoming ready; editor warmly approves of it,—Maynooth pupil this editor, a burly thick-necked, sharp-eyed man;—couldn't *be* a priest; in secret counterworks M' Hale, as I can see, and despises and dislikes his courses and him. "Give them light:" no more a *Protestant* act than that "Maynooth grant."

If the devil were passing through my country and he applied to me for instruction on any truth or fact of this universe, I should wish to give it him. He is *less* a devil, knowing that 3 and 3 are 6, than if he didn't know it; a lightspark tho' of the faintest is in this fact; if he knew *facts enough*, continuous light would dawn on him, he would (to his amazement) understand what this universe *is*, on what principles it conducts itself, and would *cease* to be a devil!—Workhouse, well enough for *it*,—" human swinery;" can't be bothered looking much at any more of them. Model-farm or husbandry school; can't find time for it,—sorry. " Piscatory school," means only school *for* fishermen's children: in the Claddagh,—whither now, past old sloop lying rotting in the river, along granite quays, government works, (hives *without* bees); and enter the school at last, and there abide mostly. Good school really, as any I saw, all catholics,—can't speak English *at first*," " Dean Burke" not there, over in England; substitute, with undermaster and d⁰· mistress, handy Irish people, man and wife if I remember; geography &ᶜ·, finally singing: and substitute goes out with us, " show you the ' Claddagh.' " Complexity of silent narrow lanes, quite at the corner of the town, and clear of it, being over the river too ; kind of wild Irish community ; or savage poor republic trying still to subsist on fishing here. Dark, deep-sunk peeple, but not naturally bad. We look into many huts; priestly schoolmaster, a brisk frank clever kind of man, knows Irish, seems to be free of them all. Petticoats, as usual, high-dyed, however dirty; lilac, azure, especially red. Old woman at a live coal of languid turf; likes "tay;" net-weaving (tho' not entirely) is going on too: husbands all out at the fishing. The herrings are still here ? "*Yes*, your riverence."—Hope they *stay* till you get *ready* to catch them!" he answered. Claddagh as like Madagascar as England. A kind of charm in that poor savage freedom ; had lately a rev^{d.} senior they called their " admiral " (a kind of real *king* among them), and priests and reverence for priests abound. —Home to our editor's lodgings now, (inn uninhabitable for assize tumult): one "Councillor Walker" has been inquiring twice for me (edit^r has told me); I cannot yet recollect him for *Petrie's*, and A. Sterling's "Chambers Walker" near Sligo, nor try much to make him out at all.

Hospitable luncheon from this good editor, Duffy's *sub*-editor now, I think;—in great tumult, about 3½ p.m. in blazing dusty sun, we do get seated in the "Tuam Car," quite full and,—Walker recognising me, inviting warmly both Duffy and me to his house at Sligo, and mounting up beside me, also for Tuam this night,—roll prosperously away, Duffy had almost rubbed shoulders with Attorney General Monahan; a rather sinister polite gentleman in very clean linen, who strove hard to have got him hanged lately, but couldn't, such was the *bottomless* condition of the thing called "Law" in Ireland. Long suburb again, mostly thatched, kind of resemblance to "the Trench" near Dumfries. Bad seat mine, quite *under* driver's, won't admit my *hat*, or hardly even my head; Walker politely insists on exchanging when the horses change. Talk, talk from W^r· very polite, conciliatory, rational too, not very deep. Bare country; not quite so stony as the morning's, not quite so barren either. Romantic anecdote (murder,? ghost,? or what) of a family that lived in some bare mansion visible to the left,—totally forgotten now. Country flattens, gets still more featureless; "John of Chume's" Cathedral tower; "little influence John of Chume;" anecdotes of some Roman-Irish Bishop and him;—Tuam itself, happily, and dismount, about 7 p.m.; reverence of landlady to Duffy; tea, Walker joining us; walk out, Mc Hale's big not beautiful Cathedral (towers like *pots* with many *ladles*); back of Mc Hale premises, "College" or whatever he calls it, outer staircase wants parapet; ruinous enough,—this *is* S^t· Jarlath's, then,? If we go into the street the protestant bishop's house stands right opposite too. Across then to protestant cathedral; old, very good, —don't go in. Ancient Cross, half of it, is *here*, other half (root or basis of it) is at Mᶜ Hale's standing on the open circuit there: " Judgment of Solomon has not answered for *these* two mothers!" On emerging, a crowd has gathered for Duffy's sake; audible murmur of old woman there, " Yer hanar's wilcome to Chume!" Brass band threatening to get up, simmering crowd in the street; a letter or so written; get off to bed,—high up mine, and not one of the *best* in nature!

Saturday 28 July.

Ostlers, horses, two rattling windows, finally cocks and geese; these were one's lullabies in " Chume;" outlook on the ugly Mᶜ Hale Cathedral, and intervening lime-patched roofs, at present moist with windy rain :—poor Duffy in his front "best bedroom," hadn't slept at all. Hurried breakfast in the grey morning 7 a.m, Bill—n. b. Bill came to us at *Sligo*, unsettled still the innkeeper said,—and Duffy with surprise paid it there too, uncertain whether not a second time ! Walker is out, bound for Sligo at an after hour; appoints us thither for Monday evening. Squabbling of lady passenger about being cheated of change by some porter or boots :—confused misarrangement and noise more or less on all hands, as usual; windy scotch-mist, coming down occasionally in shower; off at length, thank Heavent towards Castlebar and Westport, *taliter qualiter*. Watery fields, ill-fenced, rushes, rubbish; country bare and *dirty*-looking; weather rather darkening than improving. Simple big Irishman on coach-roof beside me; all in *grey-blanket*, over all; some kind of corn or butter trader, I suppose; as well-dressed kind of natives are very apt to be. "Father has *taken* the Ballina workhouse contract" said one, (who got up, farther forward on the road) : " taken it," Indian-meal at so-and-so. There is something entertaining too in a region of *unadulterated* professed ugliness? Ride by no means uncomfortable in the scotch-mist (wind to *left* and *rear*), with outlook over ill-tilled bare and ragged expanses, road flanked sometimes with beggarly scotch-firs.

Man holding up a fiery peat in a pair of tongs; stop to change horses; fiery peat is for the guard, who leans forward with (dodeen) pipe, *good-natured* gorgon-face, weighed down with laziness, age and fat: smack, smack! intense sucking, 'bacco being wet, and the saliva came in dew-drops on the big outcurled lips; poor old fellow, he got his pipe to go at last, and returned the tongs and peat by flinging them away. What a pre-established harmony, this of the fiery peat and the gorgon guard! Bright thro' the scotch-mist of the future, this fiery peat gleams beacon-like on his soul, there burns for him a little light of hope. Duffy is inside, lady passenger (of the cheating boots), and some poor young gentleman with the bones of his leg broken. Perhaps we didn't change horses at the fiery peat; but only delivered and received parcels there? Next halt, there was a change; a great begging too by old sybil woman, a mounting of one or more (grain-dealing?) passengers, with fine dresses, with bad broken umbrellas. The morning is getting wetter; stormful, dashes of heavy showers as we approach Castlebar, road running, and *red* streamlets in the ditches on either side. Duffy has proposed that we shall *stop* at Castlebar, and give up Westport; overruled. "Hollymount," pleasant-looking mansion, with lawns and groves on the left; letter to the owner, but didn't think of delivering it.

Lord Lucan's close by Castlebar and on the other side of it too: has *cleared* his ground (cruel monster! cry all people); but is draining, building, harrowing and leasing; has decided to make this ugly land *avail*, after clearing it. Candour must admit that *here* is a second most weighty consideration in his favour, in reference to those " evictions." First-rate new farmstead of his, Scotch tenant (I think), for peasants that will work there is employment here; Lord Lucan *is* moving, at least, if all others lie motionless rotting; Castlebar in heavyish rain; town-green; confusion of confusions, at the edge of that, and looking down the main street, while they tumble the luggage, re-arrange themselves, put out the poor broken-legged gentleman at the hospital— (rain now battering and pouring), and do at last dash forth towards Westport.

Wind and rain now right ahead, prefer this to stew of inside; Lord Lucan's husbandry seen to each side from under umbrella,—with satisfaction, tho' not unmixed. Gigantic drain; torn thro' a blue *whinstone* range of knolls, and neatly fenced with stone and mortar; drippings of the abominable bog (which is all round, far and wide, ugly as chaos), run now thro' it as a brown *brook*. Abominable bog, thou *shalt* cease to be abominable, and become subject to man! Nothing else worth looking at; dirty hungry cottages, in groups or single; bog generally, or low-lying rushy wet ground, with a storm of heavy rain beating it,—till certain heights, which over look Westport. Gorgon guard's face pours water from every angle,—careless he, as if it had been an old stone face:—talks busily, nonsense, what I heard of it, with some foolish passenger the only one now. Distressed gigs; one distressed gig; riders and it running *clear* with wet. Tobacco remains to one! Heights at last; Westport big substantial-*looking* (*Fronti nulla fides!*); "Croagh Patrick" big mountain cone amid tumbling cloud masses, glimpses too of the bay, all close at hand now; and swiftly down hill we arrive, get to our inn (flaring hôtel, fit for Burlington Street by *look*), and, in about ¾ of an hour of confused waiting and vicissitude, *get* our luggage, and begin to think of *seeing* the people I had letters for. Waiter despatched accordingly; people gone, people &c—One little captain Something, an intelligent commonplace little Englishman (just about to *quit* this horrid place, and here for the second time) does attend us, takes us to Westport workhouse, the wonder of the universe at present.

Human swinery has here reached its *acme*, happily: 30,000 paupers in this union, population supposed to be about 60,000. Workhouse proper (I suppose) cannot hold above 3 or 4000 of them, subsidiary workhouses, and outdoor relief the others. Abomination of desolation; what *can* you make of it! Outdoor quasi-*work* : 3 or 400 big hulks of fellows tumbling about with shares, picks and barrows, "levelling" the end of their workhouse hill; at first glance you would think them all working; look nearer, in each shovel there is some ounce or two of mould, and it is all make-believe; 5 or 600 boys and lads, pretending to break stones. Can it be a *charity* to keep men alive on these terms? In face of all the twaddle of the earth, shoot a man rather than train him (with heavy expense to his neighbours) to be a deceptive human *swine*. Fifty-four wretched mothers sat rocking young offspring in one room: *vogue la galère*. "Dean Bourke" (Catholic Priest, to whom also we had a letter) turns up here: middle-aged middle-sized figure, rustyish black coat, hessian boots, white stockings, good humoured, loud-speaking face, frequent Lundy-foot snuff;—a mad pauper woman *shrieks* to be towards him, keepers seize her, bear her off shrieking: Dean, poor fellow,

has to take it "asy," I find,—how otherwise?
Issuing from the workhouse, ragged cohorts
are in waiting for him, persecute him with
their begging: "Get along wid ye"! cries
he impatiently, yet without ferocity: "Doun't
ye see I'm speaking wi' the gintlemen!
Arrah, thin! I don't care if ye were dead!"
Nothing remained but patience and Lundy-
Foot snuff for a poor man in these circumstances. Wherever he shews face, some
scores, soon waxing to be hundreds, of
wretches beset him; he confesses he dare
not stir out except on horseback, or with
some fenced park to take refuge in: poor
Dean Bourke! Lord Sligo's park, in this
instance. But beggars still, one or two,—have
climbed the railings, got in by the drains?
Heavy square mansion, ("1770" architecture): Lord Sligo going to the Killeries, a
small lodge he has to the south—no rents at
all: I hear since "he has nothing to live
upon but an opera-box;" literally so (says

Milnes),—which he bought in happier days, and now lets.—" Croagh Patrick, won't ye go to it?" Bay.—Clew bay, has a dim and shallow look, hereabouts; "beautiful prospects."—yes Mr Dean; but alas, alas! Duffy and I privately decide that we will have some luncheon at our inn, and quit this citadel of mendicancy intolerable to gods and man, back to Castlebar *this* evening. Brilliant *rose-pink* landlady, reverent of Duffy, (proves to be a sister, daughter perhaps, of the "Chume" one) is very sorry; but—&^{c}. No *bells* in your room; bell often enough broken in these sublime establishments of the west of Ireland. Bouquet to Duffy;—mysteriously handed from unknown young lady, with verse or prose note; humph! humph!—and so without accident in now bright hot afternoon, we take leave of Croagh Patrick—(devils and serpents all collected there—Oh why isn't there some Patrick to do it now again!) and, babbling of "literature" (not by *my* will), perhaps about 5 p.m. arrive at Castlebar again, and (for D's. sake) are reverently welcomed.

Tea. Irish country priest,—very soft youth, wonderfully like one of our own green parsons fresh from college, the only one I saw of that sort. Out to the Inspector's, Captn Something, for whom I have a letter: Strelezki there, whom we had seen at Westport too, talk-talking with his bell-voice, and unimportant semi-humbug meaning: "Strelezki is coming!" all the natives, with inconceivable interest, seemed whispering to one another; a man with something *to give* is coming!—This Captn, in his dim lodging, a considerably more intelligent young man (30 or so); talk—to breakfast with him tomorrow.

Westport Union has £1100 a-week from Government (proportion rate-in-aid), Castlebar has £800, some other has £1300 &c. &c., it is so they live from week to week. Poor-rates, collectible, as good as *none*. (£28. 14 £0. say the books); a peasant will keep his cow for years against all manner of cess-collection; spy-children, tidings run as by electric wires, that a cess-collector is out, and all cows are huddled under lock and key,—*un*attainable for years. No rents; little or no *stock* left, little cultivation, docks, thistles; landlord sits in his mansion, for reasons, except on *Sunday:* we hear of them " living on the rabbits of their own park." Society is at an *end* here, with the land uncultivated, and every second soul a pauper.—" Society " *here* would have to eat itself, and end by cannibalism in a week, if it were not held up by the rest of our empire still standing afoot! Home thro' the damp streets (not bad streets at all, and a population still partly *clothed*, making its Saturday markets); thimbleful of punch over peat fire or ashes, whiff of tobacco, and bed.

Sunday 29 July.

Breakfast with Captn. *Farrar* (that was the name) sharp, distinct, decisive young soldier; manfully or patient and active in his hopeless position here. On my return Duffy has been at *mass* and sermon. Priest reproving practices on " patron days " (pilgrimages &c. which issue now in *whisky* mainly), with much good sense, says Duffy. Car to Ballina —(*Bally* is place, *vallum*); drivers, boots &c. busy packing. Tuam coach, (ours of yesterday) comes in; there rushes from it, *shot* as if by cannon from Yorkshire or Morpeth without stopping,—W. E. Forster![8] very blue-nosed, but with news from my wife, and with inextinguishable good-humour; he mounts with us almost without refection, and we start for Ballina; public car all to

[8] The present Chief Secretary for Ireland.

ourselves; gloomy hulks of mountains on the left; country ill-tilled, some *un*tilled, vacant, and we get upon wide stony moorland, and come in sight of the desolate expanses of " Lough Con."

Police-barrack, excise-barrack, in a loop of the mountain washed by the lake. Picturesque sites, in nooks and on knolls; one ruined cottage in a *nook* (belongs to Lord Lucan), treeless yet screened from winds, nestled among the rocks, and big lake close by: why couldn't *I* get it for a hermitage! Bridge (I think there must have been), and *two* Loughs. Inexpressible solitude, unexampled desolation; bare grey continent of crags, clear sea of fresh-water,—some farms and tufts of wood (one mournful ruined-looking place, which was said to be a burying-ground and monastic ruin) visible far off, and *across* the lake always. Clear blue sky, black showery tempests brewing occasionally among the hills. Brother car meets us, brief dialogue, among the crags; little pugnosed Irish figure in sunday clothes, had been escorting a comrade, mounts now beside Duffy,—proves to be a tailor, I think. Account by him, inexpressibly vague, of certain neighbouring localities. "Arch[b.] M[c.]Hale," John of "Chume" was born hereabouts, peasant-farmer's son. Given a vivacious greedy soul, with this grim outlook vacant of all but the eternal crags and skies, and for reading of life's huge riddle, an Irish Mass-Book only,—one had a kind of glimpse of "John of Chume;"—poor devil, after all! Ballina; immense suburb of thatched huts again; solid, broad, unexpectedly handsome main-street; corn-factors, bacon-factors, land agents, (attorneys, in their good days must have done it); halt at the farther end, close by a post-office, and a huge hungry-looking hôtel, or perhaps two hôtels; into one of which, the wrong one surely if there was a choice, we are ushered, and in the big greasy public room find a lieu^t of foot busy smoking.

" Private room " very attainable, but except for absence of tobacco not much more exquisite; in fact this poor hôtel was the *dirtiest* in our Irish experience; clearly about *bankrupt;* as one would see; but the poor waiters, the poor people all, were civil; their poverty gave them even a kind of dignity,—the grey-bearded head waiter's final *bow* next day (disinterested bow) is still pathetic for me. Certain Hamiltons, inspectors; the Captain H. an Ulster man; big cheeks and black *bead*-eyes; Calvinist-philanthropist; a really good, but also really stupid man. Write in my back bed-room; annoyed by gusts of *bravura singing* (Sunday not the less) from the Lieu^t of Foot; sorrow on him, and yet pity on him! To workhouse, to workhouses, with Bead-eye; *Subsidiary* workhouses these; boys *drilling,*—discharged soldier: one of the drill-serj$^{ts.}$, begs for something of the nature of "shoes" when it is done. "There is Cobden, you see!" said poor bead-eyed Hamilton; "discharged that man, and now he comes upon *us!*" Kindness *à la* Exeter Hall; this, with strict Calvinism for life-theory is H'ˢ· style. A *thatched* subsidiary workhouse this; all for the children :—really good, had the children been getting bred towards anything but *pauperism!* pauperism in geometrical progression. Dinner of perhaps 500 of them, girls I think. "Och, Sur, its *four years* I've been here, and this little girl isn't well, yet!" Four years: what a kindness to us, to stay so long! What she now wanted with this girl? "To get her taken to the salt water," —a small allowance for that. Brutallest stupidity can hardly be more brutal than these human swineries had now grown to seem to me. Dormitories &ᶜ,—a street nearly all in ruins beside this admirable place; population of it gone to workhouse, to England, to the grave.—Other subsidiary workhouse; *continents* of young women; really whole big roomfuls of them (for it was now raining) waiting for dinner.—Home with disgust; to have tea with Hamilton in the evening at his house.

After dinner, walk towards his house; moist windy evening, rain has ceased. Correct little house, good and hospitable man,—tries to convince me of philanthropy;—pauses horror struck:—I decide (in my own mind) that the *less* of this the better; he (I found afterwards) asks Duffy privately—"if I am an atheist or what?" Hospitable promise to go and show us a "country of evictions" on the morrow; we shall see! and so home to bed. It was going towards his house that a man (Sundayed workman) caught Duffy's hand, and reverently shook it with apologies.

Monday 30 July.

Worst of Irish beds, worst of Irish nights, (noise &c.) does finally end. At breakfast Hamilton is punctual and appears: "not me, thank you kindly" and the rest also didn't go,—or only Forster of the rest, and at some other hour. Thro' the streets with my two inspectors (Hamilton and his cousin the "Belmullet" inspector, a simple watery man with one arm, Mrs. Dr. Evory Kennedy's brother), towards the workhouse. "The Scotch Shop," so called; a Glasgow thing, has propagated itself hither from Sligo; dull Scotchman, "never so bad a trade as *now;*" building, furnishing of workhouses, always some money going till now; his brother has taken a farm hereabouts, (rent seemed *high* with such pauperism);—his shag tobacco (nearly unknown in Ireland) is very dear and very bad; adieu to the Scotch shop, and him! Dulse in Ballina street market;—comes from Belmullet, I hear; gathered there, carted hither, 42 miles, sold for 2/ here! wretched huckster, who has no better industry, subsists his garron upon the way side, lodges with some fellow-poor man,—goes his 84 miles, on these terms, and takes to gathering new *dulse*. Was such industry ever heard of before in this world? Not this poor huckster is to blame for it, first of all; not he first;—Oh Heavens, innumerable mortals are to blame for it; which quack of us is *not* to blame for it?—Look into the *areas* of the workhouse with bead-eyed friend; then, for his sake and for my own, I decline to go farther; return to inn,—where at least is a sofa, where tobacco and solitude are possible. Car is to go about two o'clock, and I am due at Sligo to-night. Duffy, finding certain "Dillons" here, decides finally to stay; Forster too stays, flying about in an uncertain way. Co¹· Something, a great "exterminator" hereabouts, and a great improver also; that is he, riding into town: stubborn, uncultivated big redhaired face, and solid military figure, from 50 to 60;—not the worst of Ballina men he. Glimpse of Bourke, with note from somebody, (from the Tralee gentleman it was, who had been "absent at Valentia"),—glimpse of Duffy and Dillons; away, then, away!

First part of our route, moory, at first some symptoms of plantation and improvement, by and bye none: Co¹· Something (Gort's?) evictions, long ghastly series of roofless cottages visible enough;—big drain, internal, was not visible : poor groom sitting by me on the car was eloquent as to Co¹ˢ "cruelty"; Co¹· himself, I understand, asserts that his people went away voluntarily, money and resource being wholly run out. Beggar cottagers need to be supported by public rate; whether the rate is paid them in cottages or in workhouse is really not so material as the second question " what becomes of their land, they having *ceased* to cultivate it ? Gort and Lucan answer ? Their land becomes *arable*, will be ploughed in all coming years ! Not so bad, surely— My groom gets off; *his* master most humane thrice-excellent old Dublin gentleman, driving up now with son-in-law, daughter &c. in gig; " no evictions" there, no, no ! Son-in-law, fat young gentleman, had a dish-hat as usual,—dish-hats drab-colored, black, brown, and even green, universal wear of young gentlemen here, and indeed in all country parts (Scotland and England too) at present. Flat, flat, waste of moor ; patches of wretched oats—then peat bogs, black pools; the roofless cottages not far off at any time. Potatoes,—poor cottier digging his little plot of them, three or four little children eagerly " gathering " for him : pathetic to look upon. From one cottage on the way side, issue two children *naked* to beg; boy about 13, girl about 12, " naked " literally, some sash of rag round middle, oblique-sash over shoulder to support that, stark-naked would have been *as* decent (if you had to jump and run as these creatures did) and much cleanlier. *Dramatic*, I take it, or partly so, *this* form of begging: "*strip* for your parts, there is the car coming!" Gave them nothing.

Stage: " Dromore " (?) little hamlet; country alters here, sun too is out, beautiful view of the sea, of Sligo bay with notable mountains beyond, and high (limestone) dry hills on our right too; much indented coast, circuitous road for Sligo; but decidedly a pleasant region, with marks of successful cultivation everywhere, tho' still too *treeless*, (and full of *beggary* below board, as we afterwards found). Small young lady from Dromore going on visit to Sligo, her parasol a little interrupts my view, " bay of " something ("Ballisadare" it would seem) on this side of Sligo Bay : high fine hill between the two,—north side of that, it turns out, is Walker's house. Sligo at last; beautiful descent into it, beautiful town and region altogether. Down, down, to the river-bank then halt a little to right; Mr. Walker, with servant and nice neat car is waiting: how charitable to the dusty heart-broken soul of a pilgrim from his car! No host can do a kinder thing, than *deliver* a poor wretch in these circumstances, save him from porters, inn-waiters, and the fatal predatory brotherhood!—up, some three miles; then on a pleasant shelf of the big hill or mountain " Knocknarea" dividing Sligo from the other bay, a trim fertile little estate, beautifully screened and ornamented (or soon about to be so), a neat little country house, and elegant welcome: thanks, thanks! Elaborate dinner, however, *no* dish of which *dare* I eat; salmon, veal, lamb, and that is *all!* Cold beef supplies every want. Excellent quiet bedroom; to bed utterly done, almost sleeping for an hour before I got away.

Friday 31 July.

Fine morning, fine outlook over Sligo, bay, city, mountain; around *us* pretty walks and garden, with farm improvements fast progressing, behind us the mountain rises trim and green, on the top of it an ancient *cairn*, conspicuous from afar,—which Petrie asserts gravely to be the " Grave of Queen MAB,"—some real old Irish " queen " who had grown in the popular fancy to be this! Good Petrie, he is much loved here, but there was no chance of warning him of *me* in time. —Drive to Sligo now, find Duffy and Forster just arrived, and eating luncheon at their inn, go along to visit workhouse, to visit Lough Gill: they two to dine with us at night. — Whether Duffy went with us to Lough Gill ("Wynne" of Hazlewood) I don't recollect; rather think yes; but if so he staid behind us, and came up with Forster? [Important indeed!]—Dinner was altogether polite and pleasant; Forster went about 11; then bed, and hospitable Walker will have us in town before six to-morrow, on our road towards Donegal, where these tourings are to *end*.

Beauties of "Hazelwood" (where Forster *meets* us in a car of his own) are very considerable; really fine lake (the Lough Gill itself), wide undulating park, umbrageous green-swarded, silent big house, pleasure boats on lower *arm* of Lough, and queer little windmill pump; very good indeed. "Wynne Esq"; who has this day been stirring up a row among the butter merchants, breaking *their* monopoly, and stirring up their noise. His tenants complained, "6^d per lb. a dreadful price:" get your firkins ready, full of *good* butter and *I* will give you real Liverpool prices : *hinc lachrymæ*, what the issue was, I never heard.—Of workhouse, 1800 strong, say nothing : heavy fat-flabby but solid English ex-military man for manager ; wide (idle-looking) school : group of wandering gentlemen ; one (of Rathmullen on Lough Swilly to whom we had a letter, a dark-yellow, lean long figure ; "most anxious" &c. *if* we will come ; but till Saturday he cannot be at home, and none knows whether that will answer.—Sligo and cholera ? *Telluric* or atmospheric the influence : by no means a *dirty* town ; the reverse *in comparison*. Talk of the "Cevigna mines" rich in coal and iron, say *richest;* not worked, company once, 1st manager,—*shot ;* second manager sent to Chancery ; mines sleep till "Government" make some canal or do something. Relief works in Sligo ; steep street a little levelled ; what to do with the *mould ?* Throw it into the river ! "Upon *my* salmon ? " eagerly

objects one. It is at last *carted* far away.—
Elder Walker one of the Presentment justices in relief time ; we voted away £28000 *one* morning ("English have plenty of money"); terribly indignant now that they should demand payment of *one half* of it ; "had we known that!"—a miserable business this of the famine works and relief works altogether ;—sad proof that in Ireland is *no* organic government, and in England no *articulate* d°: a d° presided over by Lord John Russell only and the element of parliamentary palaver !—Part of Sligo belongs to Lord Palmerston; I didn't learn, or ask, which part.

Wednesday 1 August.

Up at five, forwarded in all ways by kind hospitable Walker, (to whom, farewell kindly), car at the car-stand in Sligo, before six of the sunny morning.—" Gavogne" (dammed up here?) gurgling past as a considerable stream, and breweries &c. on the other side. Beggars, beggars; only industry *really* followed by the Irish people. " For the love of God, yer hanar "! " &c. &c. " Wouldn't it be worth your consideration, whether you hadn't better drown or hang yourselves, than live a dog's life in this way?" They withdrew from me in horror; did at least withdraw! Judicious confusion of loading luggage; Car full to overflowing: Sligo wit—" Go home, and shave yourself!" "Sure, I'm not so ugly as you, shaved or not!" (Fat gross fellow,—some bacon-dealer, I suppose, got this wit-arrow, ohone!) away at last; all jammed together;—steep ups and downs; horses hardly *can*, won't at one place, and we have to dismount. Bacon-dealer next me, Duffy on my right, tall old cleanly peasant jammed under Forster and driver beyond; Sligo bay, and bright sea, with moory mountainous capes in front of *us*. Lord Palmerston's country; *some* draining visible; *much* had been heard of; ugly, bare, moory country; would one were out of it all, as we now soon shall be! Donegal mountains blue-black over Donegal bay far westward to Teelin head. Dingy desolate looking country, in spite of the fine, calm morning. "Killibegs," and some coastguard station, the only sign of inhabitancy. Cleanly peasant, at sight of some new locality "breaks out into narrative; is, at least was, a coastguard,—had *once* a notable adventure, seizing or trying to seize some smuggler there,—minute particulars of it,—for 30 years seems to have done nothing else but merely "look out", the one peopled point in his old memory. Particulars from him of coastguard discipline and ways; well-done excise; when a thing is to *be* done, it can be done.—Bathing lodgings, getting ruinous many of them, (potatoe-failure has stopped supplies), good shore for bathing, and individuals, (to one's envy) are now seen swashing about in the act; blue brine and sandy shore, &c·: in Leitrim county; said once, for a moment, to be "in Fermanagh" (mistake probably?). Ruined Castle (where?) "Four Masters" did their compilation there; recollect the old black hulk of ruins,—think it might be in Donegal county further on. Bathing hamlets, d°· houses, lodges (*once* ornamental); lime and whitewash, very abundant, cannot hide ruin. "Bundoran" cleanish high-lying village, headquarters of bathing; bacon-dealer—runs to see a sick friend, Car waits for him; drink of water? *Effort*, by shopkeeper or car clerk,—think I got it, tho' after despairing. Sea and Donegal and Killibegs abroad, moory raggedness with green patches near, all treeless,—nothing distinct till steep narrow street of "Ballyshannon;" mills, breweries, considerable, confused, much white-washed country town. Breakfast, as if for the King's hundred, near the higher end. Tourists, quasi-English, busy at our table already: silent exc$^{t\cdot}$ waiter, doing his swiftest in imperturbable patience and silence. Car gone; we have to climb the steep, at the top it will wait for us. And so to the road again, quitting Ballyshannon; only Duffy, Forster, and I, of our car, did breakfast there.

Day now growing hotter, road dustier; remember nothing or little till Donegal: a M$^{r\cdot}$ Hamilton (?) has embanked some lagoon, saved many acres, gives real symptoms of being busy as a king of tillers in that quarter. Country improving; hedges even, and some incipiencies of wood shelter and ornament. Donegal a dingy little town; *triangular* market place; run across to see O'Neill's old mansion; skeleton of really sumptuous old castle,—*Spanish* gold, in Queen Elizabeth's time, had helped: by one of the three *angles* (there is a road by each) we got away again; dropping Forster who will see the lagoonembanker (didn't find him), will then by Glentier to Gweedore, and meet *me* there; Duffy is for Derry, and we part at Stranorlar; I, by appointment, am for Lord George Hill's, and have a plan of route from Plattnauer.—Bare miserable country; dingy Donegal has *workhouses* building, *pitch* employed there, no other masonry; *sleepy* valley with some trees and green patches spreading up into the sleepy mountains; high ground towards Gap of Barnesmore becomes utter peat. Barnesmore I remember well; nothing of a "Gap" to speak of; Dalveen Pass, and several unheeded Scotch ones, far surpass it in "impressiveness:" important military pass, no doubt. Moor, moor, brown heather, and peat-pots, here and there a speck reclaimed into bright green,—and the poor cottier oftenest gone. Ragged sprawling bare farm-stead, bright green and black alternating abruptly on the grounds and no hedge or tree; ugly enough,—and now from the moor-edge one sees " Stranorlar" several miles off, and a valley mostly green, not exemplary for culture, but most welcome here. Down towards it,—Duffy earnestly talking, consulting, questioning; pathetic, as looking to the speedy *end* now. Down into the valley; fat heavy figure, in grey coarse woollen, suddenly running with us, sees me, says "all r-ight!" It is poor Plattnauer, who has *come* thus far to meet me! we get him up; enter through the long outskirts of " Stranorlar," up its long idle-looking street, to coach-stand;—and there Duffy stretching out his hand, with silent sorrowful face, I say Farewell, and am off to Plattnauer's little inn; and consider *my* tour as almost ended. After an hour, of not very necessary waiting, (lunch smoking &c. provided by the kind Plattnauer) we get the car he has hired for me from Letterkenny, and proceed thither.

Fourteen miles; a tilled country mostly, not deficient here and there in wood; ragged still, tho' greatly superior to late wont; recognize the *Ulster* dialect of carman, Ulster practice of the population generally. Talk, —burdensome, had there been *much* of it? Mountains about Gweedore, details (eulogistic, enthusiastic) of Lord George Hill; three men (officialities, of some kind,—excise or other with dish-hats, before us in their car; road now rapidly winding downwards: pass them at last; can bethink of *no* other road-fellow whatever. Country greenish for most part, with gnarled crags; I should have expected ferns in the ditches, but don't remember them. Millpond at the bottom of our descent, then long slow ascent up Letterkenny Street, broad, sometimes rather ragged-looking, always idle-looking,—busy only on market days, with corn and cattle, I suppose. Hôtel at last; and carman satisfied, a grateful change into Lord George's car. To Ballyarr then! Now towards 6 or 7 o'clock. Long, mile—long straight steep ascent; then complex cross roads " to Rathmelton," to &c.; country commonplace, hill-and-dale, not quite bare; at length Ballyarr, clump of wood; high rough hedges, gates, farm-looking place; and round the corner of some offices we come to an open smooth kind of back court, with low piazza at the further side: from below piazza,—then at the back entrance, (the only handy one to his mansion) Lord George himself politely steps out to welcome us. Handsome, grave-smiling man of 50 or more; thick grizzled hair, *elegant* club nose, low cooing voice, military composure and absence of loquacity; a man you love at first sight. Glimpse of Lady (Georgina?) Hill, a nunlike elderly lady, and of one or two nice silent children; silent small elegant drawing room; a singular silent politeness of element reigns; at length refection in a little dining room, (*tea*, I suppose?)—and, in a bare but clean and comfortable room, presided over by the Great

Silences, one sinks gratefully asleep. Gweedore on the morrow like an *un*opened scroll lying before—I bethink me, we walked out too, that evening, Lord George Plattnauer and I, with pleasant familiar talk; and for *supper* after our return, he ordered me Irish stirabout, a frightful parody of "Scotch porridge," (like hot *dough*), which I would not eat and even durst not except in *semblance*. Deep ditches, *gross* kind of crop;—potatoes, turnips, "Egyptian wheat," (so called, grown from wheat found in *mummy*); land has originally been, much of it even lately, flat bog.

Monday 2 August.

Dim moist morning, pleasant breakfast (Lady Augusta (?) who has a baby, not there), paternal *wit* of Lord G. with his nice little modest boys and girls in English, German, French; Platt^r· to go with us to Gweedore. Big new mill; big peat stacks; carriage house, some 3 nice sleek wiry horses, " all kept at *work*," and able for it. Air of gentleman farmer's place and something more; car about 11 and swift firm horse, rain threatening,—which came only to a heavy Scotch-mist now and then, with brief showers. Tattery untrimmed fields, too small, ill fenced, not right in any way. Wretched puddly village, " Kilmacrennan," like an inverted saddle in site, brook running through the heart of it (?) miserable raree " caravan " stationed there, amid the dirt, poverty and incipient ruin. Road heavy and wet, past many ill-regulated little farms. Dunghill of one, " I have admonished him *not* to let it run to waste so,"—but he doesn't mind! Road (is all very obscure to me; cardinal-points, at the time, not well made out, which is always fatal to one's recollection!)—road, leading N.-westward, begins mounting, is still a little cultivated, very *steep* side road to north, Letterkenny to Glen and Carrickart I suppose!); mounts, mounts, occasional mist-rain a little heavier, day calm, and silvery, bleared glimpses had of the moor.—" National School" high up. I descend and enter, Lord George waits cheerfully, but won't; the worst of all conceivable " national schools ; " poor dreary frozen - alive schoolmaster, and 10 or 12 ragged children, — " parents take them all away in turf time;" they learn *nothing* at any time. Wrote in this book a *dis*approval. Protest against these schools ; Catholics can do little, don't always do it; a difficult affair for Mc. Donnel and Whately ! Ghastly staring "new catholic chapel," true Irish " Joss-house " on the moor to left; the image of ennui, sore-throat, and hungry vain hope of dinner ! Peat farther on ; foolish old farmer and his forces at work in peat-stack, *pack horses* instead of carts; a scandal to behold. Moor mounting ever higher, getting very black and dreary; cannot much *remember* the coming of Letterkenny and Dunfanaghy road; do remember scandalous black muddy moors, all gleaming wet as a sponge, with grey rugged mountains (*close* to us on the left), with crags, rain and silent black desolation every-where; the worst of it however I think was further on.

"Glenbeagh Bridge;" turning round a sharp corner of a muddy peat-hill, we are upon it, and see Lough Beagh, "the prettiest of all the Donegal Lakes"—no great shakes, no great shakes? Hungry improved "farm-stead" (some glimpse of slate and stone I do remember in it) with drowned meadows by the lake-side, to left. Lake narrow (outlet of it, "Owencarrow," running from left to right of *us*); high stony steep of mountains beyond it; *far* up to the left, bright green spaces, (or stripes and patches) with woods, appearance of an interesting *pass* thro' the mountains; more Highland-looking than anything I saw elsewhere; one "Forster" owns it.—At the beginning of our journey, and almost up to this point, there were large effectual long *main-drains* visible, just cut; a young Lord something's property, —sorry I cannot recal his name; he, and his "Government money" and beneficient extensive work were the most *human* thing I saw. Begins at Kilmacrenan, perhaps earlier. Here at Glenbeagh Bridge was a "relief conv$^{nc.}$ road" (very conspicuous intended-improvement, on our left), but lying as usual with a wall at each end of it. Mount again; black rocky "Dooish" (where are eagles, *seen* as we *returned* this way) on our left, and road rough, wet and uneven. "Calabber" stream (not d$^{o.}$ "bridge" (I have a distinct recollect$^{n.}$ of that; cutting down thro' the *shoulder* (you would have said,) of a considerable hill; "Halfway House," and the still heathery glen that led towards it (Calabber stream *this*, at a higher point of it, running towards Owencarrow? Alas! I had no *map* of any value; I had no time, no patience or *strength* of any kind left!) all at the half-way house, which is a coarse dark weathertight cottage, a *rebuilding* I imagine; drink for the horse; good-humoured poor woman *will* have " a drop of potheen" when you return. Lord George knows all these people; speaks kindly, some words in Irish or otherwise, to every one of them. Excellent, polite, pious-hearted, healthy man; talk plentiful, sympathy with all good in this Lord G., candid openness to it; fine voice, excellent little *whistle* through his teeth as he drove us,—horse performing admirably. After Halfway-House, view of some wretched quagmire, with a lakelet by it, and spongy black bog and crag all round, which some Irish "Dublin Lawyer" has purchased, and is improving: Lord pity him, send *more* power to his elbow! I never drove, or walked, or rode, in any region such a black dismal 22 miles of road. *This* is the road Lord George drives every week these 17 years, drives or rides, thro' these dismal moors,—strong in the faith of something higher than the " picturesque "—Mount Arrigal, a *white*-peaked very sandy mountain, *roof*-shaped and therefore conical from some points of view, beautiful and conspicuous from all (2462 feet, map says),—lay a little *west* of this Irish lawyer: we cross by the southern side of it,—and suddenly out of the black moor into view of a lake " Lough-Na-Cung ") stretching northwestward round *that* side of Arrigal; and at the head of this Lough-Na-cung, come the prettiest patch of " improvement " I have ever in my travels beheld. Bright as sapphire, both grass and woods, all beautifully laid out in garden-walks, shrubbery-walks &c. and all shrunk for us to a tidy fairy-garden, fine trim little house in it too with incipient *farms* and square fields adjoining; to our eye and imagination drowned in black desolation for 15 miles past, nothing could be lovelier. A Mr. Something's, lately deceased (to Lord George's deep regret); I think, a Liverpool Merchant (?): Widow lives here, and Lord George's doctor at Gweedore (I learn on the morrow) is to marry one of the young ladies: very well! " Lough Na-Cung " (I *heard* no name to it, but take this from the map) stretched away northward bending to west, a narrow *crescent* Lough, of no farther beauty; and from the *Clady* river, which traverses Gweedore and comes out at Bunbeg; here now *is* Lord George's domain, and swiftly descending (by the *back* of Arrigal, which hangs white-sandy very steep over us) for about a mile we are *in* said domain. " Hundred thousand welcomes!" (Irish phrase for that) said Lord George with a smile. Plattnauer and I *had* smoked our third pipe or cigar; " you can do it in 3 pipes "—*Head* of Lough-Na-Cung I remember too; stony dell amid the high mountains, mounting in *terraces* of visible rock; like some *Cumberland* pass, new to me in Ireland.

The back of the Clady, stretching out from this Lough 5 or 6 miles, and *flattening* itself wide towards the sea, is Lord George Hill's domain. Black, dim, lonely valley: hills all peat, wet and craggy heather, on each side; hills to right are quite vacant wet moor (tho' *less* craggy in appearance and lower); river-side, mostly waste quagmire of rushes, *can* become fat meadow and has here and there: river sluggish brown-coloured; hills to left (as *we* enter; hills to north, that is); are of gentlish acclivity, but stony beyond measure; sprinkled in ragged clusters here are the huts of the inhabitants, wretchedest " farmers " that the sun now looks upon, I do believe. Lord George's improvements are manifold; for instance, each man has his " farm " now all in *one*, not in 20 as heretofore, one long stripe of enclosure (dry-stone wretched wall, or attempt at wall, and cottage in or near it,) each cottage too, has now some *road;* but " improvements " all are swallowed in the chaos, chaos remains chaotic still. Hill road from " Dunfanaby," descending on the right,—not *yet* quite travellable, I think. New farm of Lough-Na-cung (Liverpool *widow*) " Improvements ;" Ulster peasant in it; has really been endeavouring; house is built, slated, stones, like a quarry, torn out everywhere, trenchings, feeblest symptoms of turnips springing, potato plot (ruined *now* alas!) is really growing; grey bony man stands looking, with what hope he can. Cottages now of Lord George's; dry-stone fence half-done along the road; has hung so for years in spite of his encouragements to get it *whole* done. Black huts, bewildered rickety fences of crag : crag and heath, *un*subduable by *this* population, damp peat, black heather, grey stones, and ragged desolation of men and things! Boat is on the river, fishy but *un*fished till now; "Gweedore inn," two-storied white *human* house with offices in square behind, at the foot of hills on right, near the river: this is the only *quite* civilized-looking thing; we enter there, thro' gateway, into the clean little sheltered court, and then under the piazza at the back of the inn, Forster waits for us, and is kindly received.

Rain has ceased, 2 pm or 3; but the air is damp, bleared, cold. Mount along the hill side; certain fields already saved out of it, not bad fields, but a *continent* of haggard crag-and-heather desolation, with its swamps and rivulets still remaining. Over the Clady something like an incipiency of a modern hamlet, and patches of incipient green; bridge thither, too far to go; chapel and school (Protestant Orange, no doubt) on this side the river; signal-staff flag now *mounted*, his Lordship being *here*, and accessible to all creatures. Dinner in our little inn. Lord George's *surgeon* (from Bunbeg; of whom mention was already) joined us, I think, in the evening. Manager of inn (for Lord George I think) an Ulster man, solid clever man of 45. Aberdeen-awa' man, chief-manager, a hook-nosed, lean slow-spoken man of like age: what do you think of these people? "Oah-h! a whean *deluidit* craiturs, Sir: but just ye-see—!" Walk, with this man in company in the evening, to the new farmhouse he is getting built for himself, and new fields he is *really* subduing from the moor; pure peat all; but lime is abundant everywhere, and he does not doubt, and will certainly prevail, he. Some 5 or 6 Aberdeen and Ulster men; nothing else that one can see of human that has the smallest real promise here; "*deluidit craiturs*," lazy, superstitious, poor and hungry. 7/6 no uncommon *rent*, 30/ about the highest ditto:—listening to Lord George I said and again said, "No hope for the men as *masters;* their one *true* station in the universe is *servants*," "slaves" if you will; and never can they know a right day till they attain that." Valley, if it were cultivated, might really be beautiful. Some air of stir and population and habitability already on it; huts, ragged potato patches, nearer there by the river side oat-patches, (lean cows, I suppose, are on the hills); *south*-side of river is as before nearly or altogether vacant of huts. Return to our inn, after arrangements for the morrow. How these people conspired to throw down Lord George's fences, how they threatened to pay no rent, at first, but to *shoot* agent if compelled, and got their priest to say so; how they had no notion of work by the day, (*came* from 8 to 11 a.m.) and shrieked over hook-nosed Aberdeen when on Saturday night he produced his book and insisted on paying them by the *hour*;—how they are in brief, dark barbarians not intrinsically of ill dispositions—talk and commentaries on all this; small close room, with the damp wind and wide moorland outside, polite "stirabout" again, to me useless: finally to bed, with pathetic feelings, gratitude, sorrow, *love* for this noble man, and *hope* as if *beyond* the grave!

Friday 3rd. August.

We drive to Bunbeg (must be far briefer to-day!) Valley spreads out into flat undulations; still crags and moor everywhere: blue sea with islands and much *sand* ahead; brisk, sunny forenoon. Visit new parsonage (Oh Orange-protestantism!); Parson, young fat Dublin Protestant, enters; has a drawing-room with "scrapbooks" and *wife-gear* (wife doesn't appear:) not a beautiful big fat young Protestant; but alas what better can be had? To Bunbeg; village (of perhaps 300 or more) scattered distractedly among the crags, sprinkled along, *thickening* a little towards Clady mouth, where are the storehouse,

mill, harbour, all amid crags forevermore!
Crag has been blasted away for *sites;* rises
yet abrupt behind the walls in that quarter,
paths climbing over it. Big excellent mill,
—proved most useful in famine time:—silent
at present, till harvest come. d^{o.} d^{o.} storehouse, or "shop" of innumerable wares;
nearly *empty* now, waiting for a "practical
shop keeper" that would undertake it. Harbour landing-place built by Ulster-man of the
inn,—"*well*-done" as I tell him. Big rings
for warping-in ships,—the General Com-
missioners of lighthouses (?) did that, after
entreaty — Aberdeen fisherman; excellent
clear-eyed brown-skinned diligent-sagacious
fellow, excellent wife of his (*before*, in a
house that wouldn't "turn rain," but was all
whitened &^{c.} and clean & hearty-looking),
from whom a drink of buttermilk for me.—
Fisherman went with us to the *old* mill and
its cascade (queer old ruin, and gushing loud
waterfall), when some of his men try the net

to no purpose.—Ancient Irish *squire* actually "begging" here; follows about in blue camlet cloak, with always some new cock-and-bull story, which Lord George, when unable to escape by artifice, coldly declares in words that he can't listen to. Strange old squire; whisky all along and late failure of potatoes have done it; gets no rent, won't sell, "a perfect pest," the fisher calls him. School, (Prot^t) better or worse,—children all *clean* at least; some 20 or more of them, boys and girls.—Sun now is *high;* we mount, turn into Bloody-Foreland road; boy on our left hand, blue water, and immensities of sand, *blown* hereabouts in great lengths over the land (as I can see from the distance,—remind me of the mansion and park *sanded*, (name?) and nothing but the *chimney tops* left, on these coasts); straggling wretched hamlet, when a fair is (monthly or annually?) go into the baker's shop (Aberdeen, he too), into a kind of tavern now under the carpenter's, where Lord George at first lodged on undertaking this affair; bare, craggy moor still, still; desolate savagery; Lord George and his Aberdeens *versus* Celtic nature and Celtic art.—Call on the Catholic priest; poor fellow, he looked suspicious, embarrassed, a thick heavy vulgar man of 45; *half* a peasant still, yet on the *way* towards better,—good growth of turnips round his cottage, cottage some approach to civilization: a book or two,—unfortunately only mass-books, directories or the like: we evidently lifted a mountain from his heart when we took ourselves away. " One man of these natives that doesn't lie." Send for him; rides with me a bit,—rough, clayey, beardy, old man, clothes dirty and bad but still whole; can't well understand him, or make myself intelligible (for he neither reads or writes) so send him away with good wishes. We are now driving, by a *back* road, towards the inn: Farm Cottage, with potato-and-corn patches as we go. "Rent," none in famine year: uncertain ever since; trifling when it does come, for nobody's rent has been raised at all: Aberdeen fisherman only clear immediate source of revenue. (*Ice*-house for him; prices now being bad *here*). People won't fish, or can't: lobster-pots given, and method shewn,—avails not. Have had to *buy* out innumerable rights, "right of fishing," "right of keeping an inn" right of &c. &c. £500. £300 &c., to keep peace, and do indubitable justice,—*after* purchasing the property. People won't work, in all or I fear the majority of cases, day's work for hire, if they have *potatoes* or other means of existing. Winged scarecrow, breaking stones (on the other road) this morning, with his scandalous ragged farm close by, is an instance: wouldn't 3 months ago; went, to some island of *Gola*, where was a cousin with potatoes and good heart; ate the potatoes out,—and *now* he works; his dress gone to the "tulip" form. May the devil pity him! —On the whole, I had to repeat often to Lord G. what I said yesterday; to which he could not refuse essential consent. His is the largest attempt at benevolence and beneficence on the *modern* system (the emancipation, all-for-liberty, abolition of capital punishment, roast-goose-at-Christmas system) ever seen by me, or like to be seen: alas, how *can* it prosper; except to the soul of the noble man himself who earnestly tries it, and works at it, making himself a " slave " to it these 17 years!?

Lunch at the hotel; inscribe in the "book;" with difficulty get packed,—roll away (Forster and all) in the sunny fresh afternoon: road seen a *second* time, not lovely still; half-way house potheen (didn't taste it, I?)—Kilmacrenan again, and fields more and more with hedges; we leaping down, had *walked* a great deal; house was excellent; but dark twilight, very cold to *us*, had now settled down; and all were glad enough to get within doors, to a late cup of Christian tea. Lord G. lights fire too, by a match; very welcome blaze: presents me two pairs of his Gweedore socks. Bed soon and sleep.

Saturday 4th August.

After breakfast, to visit a certain rough peasant farmer of the neighbourhood distinguished as being "rich." Rough as hemp, in all respects, he proved. *Sluttish*, sluttish, anxious too for "improvements," good terms to be given for reclaiming bog &c.—This was a *brother* of the peasant who had "made the money;" the latter was now dead: made by "thrift" not industry; worth little when made? A civil-natured man too; and with a kind of appetite for something cleanlier and more manful than this scene of dungheaps; poor old fellow; towards sixty, and had "tended the cows," till this *throne* became vacant for him. Home by the offices again; Lady A. with the children in the garden: a delicate, pious, high and simple lady; *sister* of Lord G's former wife. White sand (like pounded sugar) from *Muckish* mountain (I forget if this is the name that signifies "Pig" mountain—which animal one mountain does really resemble?) Proprietor wouldn't, at a *fair* rate, allow the Belfast glasshouses to help themselves to this sand; therefore they at no rate meddle with it.— Coach yoked; hasty kind farewell, and go, Lord George driving, I on the box beside him; one of the finest of days. By pleasant fields, shady or otherwise agreeable roads to Ra' Melton, or rather past the one side of Ra' Melton.—Town lying over the river, (river "Lannan," it seems); chiefly a substantial white *row* along the quay (with respectable show of ships). *Our* road (on the *west* side) being up a steep hill; wood abundant, really a pleasant active little town. Barilla manufactory (*kelp* carts passing in met us) near it; small, but precious the like of it, and rare in Ireland.

By pleasant roads still, of the same sort to Rathmullen. Old Abbey (or Castle?) there, close by the sea; quite at the end of the white, quiet, rather steep-lying village; view across Lough Swilly properly a *frith*) not bad tho' too bare. To M$^r\cdot$ Something, a retired merchant of full purse, our intended host's father-in-law. Showy, newish house and grounds, overhanging the sea near by; retired merchant not at home, his wife (poor M$^{rs\cdot}$ Sterling's dialect and manner were recalled to me) greatly flattered by Lord G's call, will give lunch &$^c\cdot$ will do all things but *speak* a little less:—we withdrew to her daughter's, to see our adventure, which doesn't look too well, to the *end*. End is: intended host has not *come*, or given any notice; will " probably " be here to-night;

help-mate, a thick, stubborn-looking lady of 40, childless, and most likely wearing the breeches, (to judge by appearances) : she invites &c.; but there is clearly only one thing, to be done,—get across to Derry, and take one's ease at one's inn. Conveyed by Lord George; meet "retired merchant" and his son; use him for getting Ferry boat secured (Ferry is *his* by county law) off, in the bright windy afternoon; a really pathetic and polite farewell from his Lordship and poor Platt$^{nr.}$ In all Ireland, lately in any other land, I saw no such beautiful soul.

Red haired ferrymen, effectual looking fellows; forts, on Irish Island &c., 5 or 6 artillerymen in each : (on Derry side); Innishowen hills on other; *bare* country as before, as *always* in this island, but with a Scotch aspect rather than Irish, beggary and rags having now become quite subordinate. Across soon; to Derry soon, by a high-lying bare, " too populous," country. Many hungry-looking clusters of cottages (slated here, but visibly *hungry*); a ruin or two; several attorneys' country-seats; (prosperous attorneys), of which the architecture was not admirable. Seven miles:—at length turning suddenly a corner, Derry is there to the south of us, close at hand; rising *red* and beautiful on elevated hill or "bluff" (it must have been once).—Foyle moderately supplied with ships, running broad and clear past the farther side of it. The prettiest-looking town I have seen in Ireland. The free school; a big old building in fields, to right of us before we enter. Two or three *mill* chimnies (*not* corn-mills all of them, a linen-mill or flax-mill one at least visible); coal-yards, appearance of real shipping trade; suburbs, gate; and steep climb by the back of the old walls; Imperial hotel in fine— "one of the best in Ireland," says report; one of the dearest, and not the best, says experience. Very indifferent bed there (wretched French bed, which species may the devil fly away with out of this British country!); and for lullaby the common sounds of an inn, augmented by a very powerful *cock* towards morning.

A D[r.] M[c.] Knight (editor, pamphleteer &[c.]) warned by Duffy, came to night; led us thro' the city wonders, the old cannon &[c.]; gave us, unconsciously, a glimpse into the raging *animosities* (London companies *versus* Derry town was the chief, but there were many) which reign here as in all parts of Ireland, and alas, of most lands;—invites us to breakfast for monday; an honest kind of man, tho' loud-toned and with wild eyes, this M[c.] Knight; has tobacco too, and a kind little orderly polite wife (a "poverty honourable and beautiful.") Surely we will go. Steamer is to sail on monday at 1 p.m. for Glasgow; Scotland ho!

Sunday 5th August.

Hot bright day; letter to Lord Clarendon (farewell, I don't *come* by Dublin), Captain Something, a chief of Engineers (surveyors, map-makers in these parts) comes to take us out to "Temple Moyle" an agricultural school, and to show us about. A clean, intelligent *thin* little soul; of Twistleton's introducing? long wooden bridge, rather disappoints, not *better* than Waterford: viewed from the other shore (height to the south, which our Captain makes us ascend) is very pretty in the sunshine. "*Grianan of Aileach*" (old Irish King's *Palace*, talked of by Mc· Knight last evening), *site* of it is visible 6 miles off to north. Good enough country, *part* well cultivated, part ill;—to London agent of Fishmongers' (? Mercers ?) Company a brisk impetuous managing little

fellow,—who escorts us to Temple Moyle;—
"M^r· Campbell" the Scotch manager, is overtaken by us on the road. Temple Moyle very good indeed, so far as *cultivation of the ground goes;* questionable perhaps, on its *human* side? A dozen of the boys, Catholics, and very ugly, were at dinner. The "teaching," our brisk Londoner indicated was rather in a staggering way. "Acre of turnips *better* than one of potatoes," testifies Campbell "and *easier* to cultivate if you do both *well*." Londoner's sad experience of Ireland; tries to promote emigrating, to buy tenants out, very sad work. "The Company's rents £4000, don't get £1500 net. If I had an Irish estate, I would sell it; if I couldn't I would give it away." Look, in returning, at the attempted futility of an "Embankment of the Foyle;" Railway to Newtown Limavaddy was to embank Foyle; £80,000 (?) spent; no railway done, none was or is *needed;* no embankment, only

s

heaps of barrows, waste flat diggings, and some small patch of ground (inconceivably small) saved out of the wreck till *new* money be subscribed. Very ugly distracted-looking flat : Home. Oh let us home ; for the evening too is getting grey and cold ! Captain to dine with us ; a weary evening,—sofa, back-garden, smoke ;—walk in the Diamond by moonlight ; respectable old city. Walker's Memorial ; Prison Gates, Bishop's House. Trade terribly gone, all say, much poverty ; Eheu ! to bed, and leave it to the gods !

Monday 6th August.

Breakfast at McKnight's : sunny hot morning,—small room full (got up the window of it, with effort !) : big Derry Protestant clergyman, Ex-mayor "Haslett;" weighty set of men. Emphatic talk to them ; far too emphatic, the human nerves being worn out with exasperation ! " Remedy for Ireland ? To cease generally from following the devil: no other remedy that I know of; one general life-element of humbug these two centuries: and now it has fallen *bankrupt:* this universe, my worthy brothers, *has* its laws terrible as death and judgment if we " cant " ourselves away from following them: land tenure? What *is* a land-lord, at this moment, in any country, if Rhadamanthus looked at him? What is an Archbishop; alas, what is a Queen,—what is a British specimen of the Genus *Homo* in these generations? A bundle of *hearsays* and authentic appetites; a *canaille* whom the gods are about to chastise, and to extinguish if he cannot alter himself! &c. &c." Derry Aristocrats behaved *well* under all this. Not a pleasant breakfast; but oh it is the last! Off to pack, and get on board.— Shameless tumult on the quays, which continued long; cattle loading, and 300 finest peasantry; Mc. Knight to take leave, and another and another; and the roar of wild men and cattle, and the general turmoil of (Irish) nature not yet ended! Yo heave ho! at last; and with many heelings and edgings (water *scant* in some places of this Frith of Foyle) we quit Innishowen Head, Malin Head, and the rest, and issue hopefully into the open sea. Bare not uninteresting coast; Glasgow Steamer going bravely, afternoon bright. Port Rush, our mooring there; last Irish crowd; Adieu, my friends, a happy evening to you. Port Rathlin Island, with many intervening rocky islets, grim basaltic.— Robert Bruce, Esq. once in Rathlin. Giant's Causeway, tourists dabbling up and down about in boats; Heaven be their comforter! We seem to be quite near it here, and it isn't worth a mile to travel to see. Poor old woman, who *has* no money for fare, shall be set out on the beach: " my son in Glasgow Hospital!" probably enough a fib; but the cabin people club, and pay her fare. Beautiful boat, but not interesting passengers,—

the reverse of that. "Fair Head" (or I forget which); combination of crags on it which they call "the Giant;" other more distant cape growing ever dimmer; and shortly, on our right, looms out high and grim the "Mull of Cantire," and we are on the *Scotch* coast! Much improved prospects, directly on opening the west side of the Mull; comfortable fenced crop-fields; comfortable *human* farms. Isle of Arran; Sandy Island? (? Beautiful blazing lights, beaming in the red of twilight); Ailsa Craig; Campbell-town bay; and now unhappily the daylight is quite gone, and the night breeze is cold; sofa in little cabin, and stony fragments of sleep. Awake, still and confused; on quarter deck are finest peasantry (hitched forward out of their place); but on the left, two cotton-mill chimnies, and Glasgow is close by. Euge! Dark City of Glasgow, pulses of some huge iron-furnace ("Dickson's Blast," so named by mate) fitfully from moment to moment illuminating it; excellent skipper, terribly straitened to land; do at last (2 a.m.) and with difficulty got into a big dark nautical Inn; no noddy, barrow or other vehicle to convey us to a hotel. Sleep in spite of all; huge mill roaring in at my open window, on the morrow at 8. Remove after breakfast; look at Glasgow (under David Hope's escort); Commercial Capital of Britain, *this;* thank Heaven for the sight of real human industry, with human fruits from it, once more! On the morrow, home by rail to Scotsbrig. The sight of fenced fields, weeded crops, and human creatures with whole clothes on their backs,—it was as if one had got into spring water out of dunghill-puddles; the feeling lasted with me for several days. *Finis* now.

This is my whole remembrance, or nearly so, of the *Irish Tour;* plucked up, a good deal of it, from the throat of fast-advancing oblivion (as I went along), but quite certain to me once it *is* recalled. Done now, mainly because I had beforehand bound myself to do it;—worth nothing that I know of, otherwise;—*ended*, at any rate, this Wednesday 16th October 1849. And now to-morrow?

THE END.

www.ingramcontent.com/pod-product-compliance
Lightning Source LLC
Chambersburg PA
CBHW031958230426
43672CB00010B/2201